# Sink

*Letting Go of Fear and Lo...*

*Beccy Mae-Rose*

YouCaxton Publications

Oxford & Shrewsbury

# Sink or Swim

Karen,
I have so much faith
in your journey ahead.
I know you will
attract your man!

Oddles of love

Beccy xx

# Dedication

My greatest wish is to leave this world a better, happier and more compassionate place because I have been here. I want this for two people more than anyone, Hannah and Olivia. Since the day I was graced to be your Mum I have always wanted better for you than I had. There might have been times where I got that so wrong, but my intention never faltered once. You have both taught me so much in your kind hearts, ability to forgive and see the best in others – even if at times not always in each other!

I promise you that I will always be there for you if ever you need me, day or night. You know you will always be my babies even if one day you choose to have babies of your own. You will always have a place to go to as long as I walk this earth. My healing might not have been pretty, but I pray that it brings the cycle of pain and hurt to a close. That you are both given the freedom to grow knowing that you are loved, always and I would never, ever turn my back on you.

Learning to be grateful for all of life's lessons and love myself full out has been hard but I hope you both learn the importance of ALWAYS believing in yourself. You can make mistakes and still be an incredible human being. Thank you for choosing me to be your Mum, it is the greatest honour and one I am grateful for every single day.

Love you to the moon and back via Pluto,

Millions, Squillions and Billions

Your Mum xxx

# Contents

# PART 1: FACING REALITY

## *Growing up with a Mentally Ill Mum*

My mum's official diagnosis is currently Bipolar.

She was very ill when I was born and her and my dad spent my childhood blaming me for her illness. Worse than all the times she would dig her nails in to me, smash my head against my bedroom wall repeatedly or push me down the stairs as a toddler (this is one of my first memories, waking up to her telling my gran I'd fallen wearing her high heels)... worse than any of the physical pain that she often inflicted on me was the constant state of fear and shame she kept me in at all times.

I could write a book about all the awful things she has done to me over the years but I don't want that. I don't want my legacy to be about her. You see she would love that because with my mum it always is about her. Because in her world there is no one else but her.

I will, however, give you a few tasters, more so that you can see if you have anyone in your life who makes you feel this way. I'm going to focus more on the behaviours now that I am an adult but key phrases she would say to me as a child were:

- You're warped - this was her favourite she told me this the most.
- This is your fault, if you weren't here I wouldn't be like this.
- You make me do this.
- You're so lucky to have me.
- You let me down, you are such an embarrassment.
- I wish you'd never been born.

- I feel everything and you feel nothing.
- I love you.

Of all of these, the one I have had to work on the most is, "I love you". At no point in my life has my mother ever shown me any love. What she has shown me is toxic abuse. To then call that love is one of the most twisted experiences. During this book I will take you through how I have recovered from this. Learnt what real love is. Healed my inner child through loving myself warts-and-all and found true gratitude for every experience I have ever had.

I say that I saved myself at 14 when I got myself moved to my grandparents and away from my parents. However, that is not totally true. Yes I got myself moved but for some reason or another I always went back to her. In fact until recent years my mum had totally convinced me that my father had abused me, so much so that I haven't seen him for over 21 years. It is incredible what someone deeply toxic can and will do to twist the reality of the people around them for their own gain. This is something called gaslighting and it is a powerful tool used by many abusers.

My need to go back is part of my own dream of having a happy and healthy family. I always wanted to look for and find the best in my mum and many others in my life. I always believed for a long time that there would be a grain of love, good, magic almost, that one day she would change and finally begin to show me love. That has never, and I now believe, will never happen. That wasn't the journey I was born to. I was not born into a loving, healthy family. I was born into a deeply toxic family and I am the one to bring that cycle to a close. This is my blessing. Not to have that love from them but to find it within myself and help others to do the same.

Here are some examples of my mother's behaviour towards me as an adult.

- She convinced me she had cancer during my second pregnancy when my grandmother was already seriously ill with an autoimmune disease and having chemotherapy. This is called Munchausen Syndrome - the need to gain attention by faking serious illness.

- She persuaded me to buy a house with her and give up my home, only to cancel our agreement the day before completion, leaving me and my children homeless. She had no remorse.

- She lied about me and accused me of stealing to the point that she was sectioned for my safety due to the extreme nature of her lies. She continued the lies after being released from hospital.

- On my wedding day, she put her hand over my wedding ring and said, "I've just got engaged". She tried to show off her ring, wore her "wedding perfume" and took photos with her fiancé by my wedding cake. I had not wanted her at my wedding but was convinced that I "had to or I would regret it". My gut was right, she had no consideration for me at my wedding at all. She had to try and make it all about her.

- She cut me out of the eulogy at my grandad's funeral and acted as if I didn't exist. Because I had become wiser to her goading me, I didn't react to her at all that day. This led to her punching her mother, a woman in her 80s and with dementia, in the face that night. She tried to make herself out to be the victim the next day claiming my gran was rude to her husband which was totally untrue.

- She told my ex-husband she thought I had bipolar and encouraged him to remove my children from me.

- She always claimed poverty so that I paid for things and rarely contributed until she felt she might be caught out, then she would offer to buy expensive gifts rather than talk about the pain she had inflicted.
- She used money as a way to try to control me. "It'll all be yours when I'm gone."

Her friends in Spain even asked me if she could be a psychopath.

All I want now is freedom from my mother. I do not ever want to see her, hear from her or about her, ever again. This could be a challenge as I am her legal next of kin and when she becomes seriously ill and needs to be sectioned it is me they will have to call. Whereas in 2017 I put my life on hold to support her following the sudden death of my stepdad - which cost me greatly in time and energy and took me away from my business and the future for my daughters and I.

Taking back my power, moving my time, energy and attention away from her and other toxic people, has been my biggest gift to myself.

My story is not about who I was born to, married to, or any court case, but about how I learnt to find the lessons and grow into a woman no longer afraid of her own light.

## Hold the Fuck On!

No matter how hard it gets, no matter what your life throws in front of you promise yourself one thing above all else... you will hold the fuck on!

Social media is full of people who transformed, who woke up differently one day. Well it wasn't that way for me and I have a feeling it's not that way for many. Healing is a spiral, I have found. Just as I think I am healed something rises up again, smacks me in the face almost to say, "You're not done yet."

Swimming through the mud of a traumatic past isn't as simple as BOOM it's all sorted. Some days it feels like you are really making headway and others you're knocked so far off your perch you wonder why you're even trying. When that day comes... if it never does for you then you are blessed. But when the day comes where it all feels too much, please hold onto your promise to hold on and not let go.

My day came like a bolt out of the blue. I was doing OK. Broke as hell but holding it together well. I had found a home for me and my girls, I had a job that just about covered the bills. I was working each day on letting go of the past and building a new future. 'Keeping my head down' I would call that phase and I was quite proud of myself. My girls were happy I'd managed to sell a few things to take them places on our staycation and I was working hard on letting go of the guilt I had about selling our home and losing my matchmaking business.

Now I'm not going to dress this up. I had 4p in my bank and £5 in my purse and 16 long days until payday. I knew I had a long way to go to have a stable life again but I had a plan. This book had been started, I had a side job in place with amazing supporters. I had a 90-day plan to get things moving in my life again. I'd pinpointed that I was happiest when I was helping others and that was my mission. That IS my mission. This is my reason for being here, to be mum to my awesome girls and to help others get through the mud of life and bloom like a lotus.

So let me take you back to my day that hit me square in the face. I was sat at my desk in this office job where the people are lovely but I can't help wondering how the hell I ended up here. The work is very repetitive and most of the time I'm bored out of my mind and the hardest part of the job is to keep focused, but I was doing it day in and day out. I never missed a day other than for holidays or if my daughters were sick. It was never going to be my path all the way out of the mess I had created around myself but it was a great place. Somewhere to hold on from.

Out of the blue the receptionist comes over and says there is someone at reception for me. I walk over and there is an air of tension. I've been behind on my bills for a while and I was wondering if it was a bailiff. Hold on, I thought, I've checked my credit rating I'm catching up and I cleared my old council tax debt just last month. My thoughts were racing and I did my best to stay calm and hope that no one in the open plan office was noticing.

As I walked over, there was a young man I didn't recognise and then an older man turned around and the recognition landed. He was the father of my old landlord. He handed me an envelope and I walked in the office foyer and asked if I had to open it there. He said "no" and then said with a really proud boastful tone, "You've been served". I headed back to my desk shaking.

When I had left my previous flat my mother had intentionally and knowingly made my daughters and I homeless. I will never forget the day that she called her solicitor and cancelled the purchase of a house that we were due to move into the next day. I had spent three months caring for her after the loss of my stepdad, and while she was mentally ill. I dropped everything for her the moment I knew she needed me. This was too much.

When we went back to the hospital, she was told by her support team that this was nothing to do with her illness and that she had chosen these actions. I was so shocked. Even after everything she'd done I had always looked for a glimmer of hope, a glimmer of good in her. She's my mum, I had a right to want her to have some kindness in her, but there wasn't any. Our meeting began to get worse. I was sat there in shock. She was then asked if the things she had said about me were true. She immediately said, "No, no, no they are 120% not true. Beccy is an amazing daughter and I couldn't wish for better." I was confused, particularly as she was then asked if she would sign to say that is the case. She agreed and began going on about something else in a very dramatic and loud manner but I couldn't hear her as my brain scrambled to process what I'd just heard.

I asked the lady in charge what was going on. She told me my mother had made some serious allegations against me and I only had one question at that point. "If you had believed my mum would you have had to call Social Services?" The wait for the answer seemed like an eternity as there is no way in the world my mum wouldn't have known that something like that would have instantly lost me my children again.

"Yes Beccy, what your mum said was so serious we would have also had to call the police."

"I can't do this," was all I could say as I got up to leave. As usual my mum was again trying to make it all about her. Screaming and shouting about something but for once I couldn't hear her at all. I was in total shock. As I walked out I tried to figure out what I was going to do. All of my things were boxed up, I had no money now and nowhere to live. I knew I couldn't see her again. I needed some time. I was told to take at least the weekend and to focus on myself and my girls. The staff said they were there to support me as much as my mum and I had to put myself first now.

When I got back to the car all I could feel was my aunt's anger. It was clear that for her this was all about her. I was shocked and in a daze. My aunt was saying how she could kill her. It was all too much for me. My aunt drove to a nearby supermarket because she was too angry to drive. I was promised that my mum would have to pay to find us somewhere. While we walked around I began to worry about my mum and how she'd seen me leaving, and I called the hospital. They said she was fine and "having her second dinner". I should have known she wouldn't have cared at all.

Well, to cut a rather long story short, my mum was sectioned the following week. As her next of kin I had to go in to say I didn't object, which of course led to me being told I'd done this to her. Both doctors assured me that they would have gone to court to displace me as next of kin had I objected.

How does this relate to me being served in my new office?

While my family had all agreed at the start that my mum would need to make up for what she had done, somehow over time that moved to, "Well you should have known not to trust your mum". As always it became my fault. Again, something I should have expected but it's natural to want to trust your own flesh and blood. You trust they will not try to actively destroy you, instead you look towards them and have faith.

One thing she had agreed to was paying the rent and the issues at the flat which were caused by me having nowhere to move to. The court paperwork was a CCJ for just under £6000. All that my mum had chosen not to pay.

Once again I had trusted her to keep to her word and as always she had done exactly what was going to cause me the most trouble. Now to put this into perspective my mum is well off. She doesn't care about anything or anyone, only herself and money. So she has multiple properties, investments, a brand new car... if she had wanted to pay this would have been no issue for her at all. Once again she chose to do this. This was not her illness. This goes back to, once again, my own mother, the one who was meant to protect me, being the biggest form of pain in my life. By now I should be surprised... yes, that message is coming through loud and clear.

The day I was served with the CCJ, I was saved by the kindness of the beautiful young lady who sits next to me at work. She is one of the reasons I began writing this book. That day she was like an angel, she said she was popping out for something and brought back £20 and told me to put petrol in my car. I don't know if I could put into words just what that did for me. This act of kindness showed me that the world is full of good, kind people. It couldn't have happened at a better time. I drove home, via the petrol station and kept my head together quite well.

The next day, however, was a different story. I woke up crying. I drove to work crying. I didn't want to take a lunch break at work because I didn't dare stop or I would cry. I felt paranoid about the help I'd been given the day before, like I'd burdened a young woman with my problems and by the time I was driving home I had decided to kill myself. All the way home I cried and I planned my letters. I planned to write to each of my girls telling them how incredible they are, that they are better and stronger than me. I planned to write another letter asking if anyone I'd ever helped or made feel better or even made smile would write to my girls and tell them the good stuff, so they could know all of the good stuff that was also in their hearts.

I thought about how I would do it. I could drive in front of a bus, others might get hurt. A train, again the pain for the driver was too much for me. I thought about taking lots of paracetamol and ibuprofen and wine but I couldn't afford the wine. I got home and I was ready to write the letters when a message came through asking if I was OK. Apologising for not being in touch. I had another on my Facebook asking if I was OK.

I spent about an hour Googling ways to kill myself and all the help numbers came up - but I had no active phone to call. I read all the ways I could do it and thought seriously about them all. Then one thought hit me, who would find me? No one knew my address and my girls were due over in a few days. I simply couldn't have them find me.

I replied to those two messages and admitted, to a point, how I'd been feeling. I did end up saying to both that "of course I wouldn't do it" but didn't admit just how close I was. Both of them asked me to promise for now was that I would hold on.

So I promised to hold the fuck on.

No matter what happens. No matter how shitty it can get I am holding the fuck on.

Healing isn't a pretty process, not for me at least, but as I now type this with my two girls chilling in the other room I am so darn glad I held the fuck on.

Have my finances changed much? No, but I did ask a friend to lend me £50 and they transferred it within the hour. I have spoken to my side job and have some support for that and I am sat here typing this knowing that last night we toasted marshmallows on a disposable BBQ, my littlest danced and we all laughed while playing a board game.

I know I don't need my 'family' because they have proven repeatedly that I am better off without them, but wow my girls do need me. You see I learnt in my holding on that I am nothing like my mum. My girls need me and whatever it takes I will come back from it all.

Whatever your version of holding on looks like. Please promise me, no, promise YOU that whatever happens you too will hold the fuck on. When holding the fuck on - and you will know when you are truly holding the fuck on - try to look for the lesson. Mine was HUGE.

I AM nothing like my Mum. My girls need me and I don't ever need the woman I was born to.

Something huge healed in that moment when I chose to hold on. Hold on too and see what you can hold on to and let go of. Tell someone, anyone, how your feel and please ask for help!

## No One is Going to Save You

I am finally able to admit that for the longest time I was in search of someone to save me.

I would find myself wondering when someone was going to step in and make it all better. I didn't just wait, I actively searched. I paid for counselling, therapy, I went to seminars, I broke boards with my bare hands, bent thick metal poles with my windpipe... yes, I thought I might end up feeling more like a chicken kebab with that one!

I found mentors, people to look up to. I watched YouTube videos. I read books, countless books. I became a self-help junkie. I even spent some time as a motivational speaker myself. There are some videos around on the internet somewhere. I loved helping others. It was and without doubt is my calling.

Here is the thing, though, I had forgotten to heal and help the one person that mattered the most. ME.

Yup I know that sounds like the most selfish phrase. But it is so true. I hadn't helped myself enough to be up on any stage trying to help others. Yeah I was good at the talking, the presenting and pulling together of an event. But I wasn't ready, I had more work to do.

Then my work fell apart and I went on my spiritual journey. I hired an energy coach. I learnt to read tarot and got crystals. I had reiki healing, crystal healing and pranic healing - all of which was brilliant and I am grateful for every element of it. I journaled. I did gratitude lists. I meditated. I let go. I forgave. I was an all-round good student.

The truth was that while I kept searching for an answer I was really looking for someone to save me. I was looking for someone to have the answer, for there to be some magical formula that made it all OK. For something to make me OK.

Yes I had friends who lent a hand. Yes I gained from almost all of the learning I did. Yes some of those YouTube videos were helpful. Most of the courses, seminars and books taught me something. I am not knocking them or denying that.

During my path I learnt a lot, vast amounts about Cluster B personalities - psychopaths, narcissists and sociopaths. I learnt how they operate with so little consideration for others and only care about themselves. Then I became so paranoid about being like them that I went out of my way to help others... and I neglected my basic needs.

This is not healthy. Nor is it long-term helpful to anyone. We all have the right to have our needs met. We all deserve a home, food, water, a life of our own. The fact that I was willing to put my mother and grandmother before myself and lose what little I still had in caring for them, was NOT a positive thing. This was a form of me not taking responsibility for my own life.

Yes, it was reasonable to expect that after supporting my family that they would, in turn, be there for me and my girls. But they were not and realistically they had never shown me any evidence that they would be. I was foolish and lacking in self-worth by putting their crisis above my own. It wasn't only them that I did this with. The day after my mum made me homeless, a friend had a family crisis and I dropped everything for her too. This was my pattern; help others and get little to nothing in return. Why? Because I didn't think I was worth it. I allowed people to treat me that way. Me going around helping others, while it could be seen as kind, was actually making me emotionally and morally bankrupt. I had nothing. How could I go around giving my time, energy and focus to others? I had a duty to myself and to my children to save myself first.

So here I am saving myself first. I am rebuilding our world piece by piece, choosing what parts of the past I decide to bring forward with us, the people who have shown us kindness and humility and the experiences that have enriched our lives. In sharing my journey I hope that it will give someone else the spark to get on with saving themselves.

Yes, it is, of course, admirable to help others. Yes, being there for others is an essential part of a rounded life BUT not at the expense of your own self.

I'd heard and said countless times that you have to put your own air mask on first, and you can't serve from an empty cup. Well, one of my lessons became finding out what that truly meant. You can give and give and give to some people and it will never be enough. They will often forget, or worse, twist all you did for them. This is not your path as much as it was not mine to give until I was drained, physically, mentally, spiritually and financially. Saving them does not mean they will ever save you.

You have to get on with saving yourself. Saving yourself on every level. You have a responsibility to save yourself. It is the biggest gift you can give anyone you love, get on with saving you so they can get on with loving you and not worrying about you. For me, swallowing my pride and getting a day job was phase one of saving myself. But it was never going to be the whole answer. I then moved out of the loveless and cold relationship that I had found myself in.

Having a job that barely covered our bills, living in a one-bedroom flat that I had to sublet because I couldn't get a normal tenancy was a huge step forwards from where I was a year ago, where I had been for the last 6 months. It was hard to live that life knowing that just four years before my life was wonderful. One of my challenges was to let go of the past and to stop emotionally battering myself with the stick of the past.

Saving myself for myself and for my girls became my biggest mission.

I finally became the hero I was looking for all along.

If you are reading this looking for someone to save you, please believe me and let me save you some of the hardship and heartache that I went to through to find it. YOU are the only one who can save you. I feel like I finally know what that line in *The Wizard of Oz* was all about: you had the power all along.

Taking my energy back from everywhere and everyone that I had been giving it to for so long was not being unkind to anyone. There are only three people on this earth who need me until my cup of energy, life and fulfilment overflows and that is me and my two awesome daughters.

I trust wholeheartedly that anyone in my life who I lose in the path to saving myself really doesn't belong in my world anyhow. I am grateful for everyone who has touched my life up until now and I trust that those meant to make it to the other side of me will.

I believe that we as humans are all broken in some way. That we all need to heal. That the greatest gift we can give, not only to ourselves but the world around us, is to swim through the mud, the dark, ugly, awful parts of ourselves and make peace with that. To stop holding it together so darn well and allow ourselves to break because I believe that in that broken mess is our whole. Our light is not found in the best of us but in making peace with the worst of us.

I am saving my own self today and every day.

Taking the time each day to allow yourself to face the darkest parts of your soul isn't an easy task. The times I have cried my eyes out aren't times of weakness, they are the times that I allowed myself to heal from things that for so long I had tried to pretend hadn't hurt. Pushing down the pain and putting on a brave face doesn't serve anyone long-term.

I know that working an office job isn't enough for me long-term but right now I am so incredibly grateful for the chance to do something that keeps a roof over our heads, clothes washed, we can have a shower whenever we want, we might not have fancy food but we don't starve. This is a great place from which to grow and heal.

Each day I do at least one meditation on either cutting the cords with past hurt and trauma, opening my heart chakra and letting hurt out and light in, forgiving or living in the flow. Each day I ensure that I take care of my basic needs and eat, take some exercise and I am grateful for all that life has brought to me. Each day I ensure that I am meeting my needs first and then if there is any left I offer that out to others. I am getting stronger each day.

Pulling my energy back from this search for someone to save me, and from the need to jump in and try to save others, has allowed me the time, space and focus to save the only person I can truly change. Me. We are all given this human experience to learn. I have learned that no one is going to save you. We each have to save ourselves.

Since I have allowed myself to connect with all that is me and accept who I am, the awesome and the awful and everything in between, I have been able to do more healing than ever before.

I have learnt to accept myself. Learnt to love myself. To trust myself and to value myself. No one could teach me those things. I had to do that work all for myself.

## The Mask of Positivity

Positive mindset is a huge thing. It is a multi-million pound business. You can't be on social media for five minutes without coming across a positive meme.

For a few years I tried to build my life and business around positivity and that if you shift your mindset then you can do and achieve more. This is in essence true.

We have all experienced being around someone who always sees the bad in things. The person who drains the energy of a whole group of people, all the time. Then we have also all met someone whose energy and enthusiasm is seemingly boundless. They are two clear and well- spoken about characters if you ever delve into the world of personal development.

For as long as I can remember, I have been told that I am the second of those people. I have been told that my energy is infectious, I am the most positive person they know and so on. For a long time I was. This was who I was. I got up each day, did my meditation, gratitude lists. Each day I shared positive memes on my social media and most of the time I meant them.

The thing is, though, that life isn't always positive. Yes a positive mindset is highly beneficial but it isn't the only answer. There are times when choosing to see the best isn't enough. There are also times where speaking to someone who is in deep pain in this way is frankly naive and harming.

No one can be positive all the time. You show me someone who claims to be and I will show you a fraud. None of us are all of anything. As much as life ebbs and flows so do our feelings and experiences. It is not healthy to push everything down to having a positive mindset and choosing to think or feel differently.

There are times when someone's pain just needs to be heard. It needs to be acknowledged. It needs to be allowed. People need to be allowed to be positive and still have a bad day. We need to be allowed to have the full range of emotions and experiences. There is nothing more insulting to someone who is trying to actually face their deep inner turmoil and face up to it than being told your story and how hard you have had it. This is not a competition. It is not important who has been through the worst experience and survived.

Asking someone who is trying to work through their shadow self and make peace with it to be positive is not only ludicrous, it is shaming. Very few people have the guts to look at the very worst of themselves and take total ownership for all that they find. If you haven't had the guts to do that yourself, you have no place in telling another that they need to be positive.

We all have our own paths that we must lead to find our own depths. For me, what I once thought was wonderful in the world of positivity, I now find a little on the shallow side. It has its place without out any doubt but it is a one-size-fits-all, off the shelf answer to the world's problems. It would be so easy if it was, wouldn't it? Oh, your life isn't going well, you should have kept your thoughts more positive.

No one is positive all the time. No one. Not even the Dalai Lama claims to be positive all the time and have you seen him? He always looks happy and at peace. Why can't it be ok to be positive most of the time or when we choose to be, yet still let off steam and have a good old moan? We all need to let that bad stuff go, let the anger, resentment, grief and frustration out of us.

While the positive emotions are the ones we look to cultivate, we cannot begin to pretend that bad stuff doesn't happen to good people and that we are all OK to feel a little broken, fed up and in need of a non-judgemental hug every now and again. When we let down the mask of positivity and allow people to see us for the full range of emotions and states that we can be, then we invite them to share with us their fears, anxieties and complexities. In these moments where we are able to share we are also able to connect and understand each other.

I am not for one second suggesting that we need to embrace full flow pity parties and excuse- making, but we cannot let our world become somewhere we shame each other for lapses in positivity. We are all human, we are all flawed and we all have bad days from time to time. Some may even have bad weeks, months and years. Learning to accept that it happens, it WILL pass and that you can share this stuff is vastly healthier than insisting on a mask of positivity.

I would much rather have a deep, genuine, flawed and passionate conversation with someone who has the guts to be real about their life. To see the pain in someone's eyes as they struggle to hold back the tears from their most recent loss or see them go red on the neck and cheeks as they tell you about the person who infuriates them to the point they want to throw something. I would much rather talk to someone with these depths than someone who just wants to talk about the most wonderful parts of the world as they see it.

Yes, please do tell me about the moments that were so wonderful you couldn't believe they was happening and least of all to you. Please do share with me the view that took your breath away, which no picture could ever do justice to. I love to hear about your one dream that you can see so clearly in your mind that you know without any doubt will one day come true. Please do tell me all of this but don't tell me it at the expense of the part of me you have been told you need to hide.

Hiding is for those who are in the kindergarten of life. If you want to graduate the university of life and dance in the true passion of your soul and get a glimpse in the wonder of my soul, please take off your mask and sit with me awhile. When someone has the courage to take off their mask and be all of them - the shame, guilt, upset and embarrassment along with the joy, excitement fun and silliness - then you know you are sitting will an old soul.

Positivity is beautiful. Positivity if fun. Positivity can put a rocket pack into your life. I know it. I have felt it and I have seen it. It is only half of the story, though.

No one is all light. No one is all of the good things. We are all both. The universe is in balance and we are too. The darker your darkness the brighter your light can shine. The more you can tell the depths of your awful, the horrors of your soul, the more you are capable of shining so brightly that you give one of the people unable to climb out of their darkness a glimmer of hope.

That is what I believe is all of our purpose. To help those who can't see past the darkness of their situation or their soul to shine our light back to them to show them the way. That is not done with positivity alone, that can only be done by showing that we have been down in that same hole too. Keep the positive mindset. Keep your drive to move forwards but don't lose the ability to take off that mask and show your darkness.

If you have yet to meet your darkness then I would be going to look for it. Invite it to come and sit with you and talk to you for a while,

21

make it your friend before it crashes into your life like a tornado, taking with it anything that gets in its way.

## Ostrich - Head in the Sand Approach

Looking back over my life, now that I have been able to accept total responsibility for everything that has happened, has shown me something I already kind of knew. I have a tendency to be like an ostrich when the going gets tough. My coping mechanism has often been to put my head in the sand.

There have been many times where that wasn't the case and I stood and faced things but there came a time when it all got too much and this was how I dealt with it.

I am working hard at not judging myself for this because in all honesty the level of awfulness I was facing was enough to warrant the ostrich method. I am quite sure that few people could stand and face all of the things I had going on. If this was what I had to do at the time to get through it, I am more than OK with that. This is not about blaming or shaming myself, this is more about accepting that this is a coping method I developed during the worst time of my life, which, in the long run didn't help me.

Adopting the ostrich method can allow space for some of the tough stuff to be ignored long enough for some tiny parts of joy, happiness or even ok-ness to come back into your life. I did go a little too far in that I didn't open my post in nearly two years. The thing with the ostrich method (and I am glad that I chose this over the alcohol, drugs, food methods of numbing my pain) is that just like the others it provides space from needing to deal with things. While some of the addiction methods can also leave physical damage this one did not.

Avoidance never ends the issues - they all still have to be faced at some point.

Accepting that at some point my head had to come out of the sand and I had to face the storm that was waiting for me (which would be worse because I had ignored it for so long) has been huge. It is not easy to stand and face the realities of all the things that got worse while you were unable to face up to the day-to-day aspects of life; the bills I didn't pay, the car I didn't get serviced, the business I stopped making sales in. It all mounted up and I had to face the realities of the consequences.

The cold and harsh truth of the world that we live in is that is it fundamentally lacking in compassion. There is compassion if you are rich enough to still cover all of your bills but if you can't keep on top of those things then you are viewed as lazy or lacking in integrity, the list goes on. I found that the more I tried to face up to the reality of the mess that had been created by my ostrich approach, and also my naive choice to trust a woman who regardless of her blood connection to me had never shown me kindness let alone love, the more I realised that in the main our world is not set up to care.

As I began to call companies to look to arrange for payment plans, most did not want to know. I found that simple errors that are more than understandable in a time of trauma such as missing a toll that used to be pay as you go over, missing £2 in a charge went up to £424.50, for each crossing and ended up costing me over £1600. My car was clamped the day I needed to be at the hospital (that was over the other side of the county) to be at my mother's sectioning meeting. The way that the bailiffs handled the situation was inhumane. There is no reasonable justification that a £2 crossing can go on to cost so much.

Yes, I do understand I had made mistakes but the outcome vastly outweighed the mistake. We do not live in a society that supports people when life gets tough, it adds pressure. This isn't fair, justified or reasonable. It might be legal but that doesn't make it ok. For someone who has a lot of money this would not be an issue. They would be able to make these errors during difficult times in their lives and the impact would be annoying. But it would not significantly impact their lives. I do not understand why we seem to think that fines are an appropriate way of dealing with minor mistakes. There is more to this life than money.

Taking my head out of the sand has meant I have had to face all the things I couldn't face before, regardless of whether I believe them to be fair or not. I can do that. I know now that I do have that strength. I also know that I had every right to be an ostrich with all that I had going on. If this then takes me a while to clear up and make good then that is my responsibility and I will do that.

My head is very much out of the sand now. I do not believe I will ever choose to go back to being an ostrich again. It served me well at the time. I dread to think how I would have reacted had I tried to cope with the practicalities, and something that at the time seemed so insignificant to me as money, alongside the things which mattered to me the most.

During this time I found that I really do value family first. While my family was in turmoil nothing else mattered other than protecting my children in the best way that I could and at that time being there for my mum and my gran. If I could go back now I am not even sure I would change that. I might reduce the amount of time and effort I gave my mum and gran as I could have used that energy more on my business and that would have kept my finances more in check.

But here is the thing, I have always believed, maybe a little foolishly that you can always earn more money. There is only one thing that you cannot get back and that is time.

I am grateful that I was able to stay by my grandad's side from the moment he needed me. I am proud that no matter what my mum has done to me I got on a plane and flew to be at her side during my stepdad's funeral. I am glad I supported her to get into hospital and receive the care she needed. When I went to pick up my mum from hospital and put her needs first even though she had made me and my children homeless, I knew then that I am everything she can never be.

When I launched the Love Summit and it needed my 100% attention but two days later my gran went into hospital and I sat with her for 18 hours a day to be sure she was OK, I would not go back and change that. There is nowhere else I would have rather been than by her side when she was scared. When the other patients commented on how lucky she was to have a grandchild who cared so much and she looked aghast that the compliment wasn't for her, I know that I was doing the right thing.

For the longest time I have always had the ability to put the needs of others above my own. I am proud of that. I am proud to have been that person who hasn't made excuses but has been there, even when there was every reason not to. It is time to take my head out of the sand and realise that there is no one who is willing to do the same for me. I know because I asked them and they refused. It's time for me to give to myself all that I have been willing to give to others, with the same degree of passion and lack of excuses.

You see my children and I can't live off the kindness I have shown others. I can, however, see me in my girls. I can see their willingness to be there for others. That makes me proud. If they have learnt kindness then all of this has been worth it.

Our summer of no money. Well, it's amazing how much fun you can have going to the park, and taking a picnic to London. I did manage to get enough money for some trips but not the huge days out and holidays away that we are used to. Not once have my girls complained. They are happy that I am here with them, that I have booked the time off work to sit and play games with them, to talk to them about their hopes and dreams.

This ostrich is ready for change. I am ready to transform into a flamingo in a flock of pigeons and stand out once again.

My time as an ostrich has taught me a lot about myself, my family, my priorities and led me to a path I never expected to walk. I am grateful for this journey and all that I have learnt. I am ready to put me and my girls first and create the life we have always wanted. One that is full of fun, laughter and memories... oh, hold on, we have done that even without money this summer.

Let's see what can be done once I am ready to begin creating, accepting and allowing again. We are worthy of more and we are ready to create it. I have forgiven myself wholeheartedly for the time I was unable to face the practicalities of life. I take total responsibility for the outcome of that time and I have a deep faith that things will work out beautifully for us.

I can once again feel the magic of the world around us and all that the universe can create with and for us. I am ready to make our world beautiful again.

## *Asking for Help*

I have never been able to ask for help.

It is my fundamental personality flaw.

Learning this and accepting it has been hard. Facing the destruction I have caused in my own life because of this was painful. I know now that I always expected others to be like me. Ready to drop everything for those I love without needing to be asked. I would step up, be there, often at the expense of my own life, my own needs. If I had it I would share it. I would give materially, and financially, and offer my time, effort, energy and focus without a second thought.

I believed for a long time that this made me a 'good' person.

I was wrong.

What this made me was a person who gave too much and didn't ask for help.

I had a lack of boundaries. I would help even when not asked to, which I still do stand by. If someone you love is deeply struggling, I still believe that love is to step up and step in for them. However, for me to expect others to do this for me, and to not articulate my needs, that is all on me. I was weak, I was flawed and I was trying too hard to be a 'good person' to dare ask for help.

The truth is I was too scared of being judged as weak, needy, and useless if I needed help. I had never experienced what it was to be helped without a side of judgement, shame or that nasty salty sniping. This comes from having been brought up in a deeply toxic family. I see that so clearly now. There are friends that would have helped if I had ever dared ask. I have been in relationships where my partner wanted to be there for me as much as I was there for them but I wouldn't let them. My inability to ask for and accept help has caused the majority if not all of the pain I have felt in my life.

I love my grandad deeply and always have. I used to say he was the only man in my life that never hurt me, but a few things he taught me did. He said that nothing should go outside of the family. So I had to pretend my mum was kind and nice so as not to bring shame on our family. I was told to get back with my ex-husband when one of my daughters acted out at nursery – she was doing this because she came from a broken home. He told me my grandma was my best friend. He was wrong on every level. A great man but he was so blinded by his love for my grandma and his daughters he couldn't see how poisonous they all were and are.

His advice kept me going back to my mum, gran, ex-husband and very occasionally my aunt. When I did turn to my grandad and ask for elderly advice he would say it was my life and I had to live it my way. I would often get upset about this and say I'd asked his opinion because I trusted him and wanted it. I wanted to bounce my ideas with someone who'd already lived. At the same time I spent years, decades even, commenting on how my gran spoke to him and that if I ever treated anyone that way I would be ashamed. Looking back now I see he was swallowed by the toxicity of his wife and daughters as much as I was.

He never asked for help.

Even as my grandad lay dying he still tried his best to put my girls and I first. We had spent the afternoon there and he never once complained. After my girls left I went back to find my gran still chirpy and fine, but my grandad wasn't in a good way. His carers were due and while he had only been on paracetamol for the whole time he was in home-based palliative care, something had changed. Something that he didn't ask for help with.

When the nurse arrived he was in so much pain I could see the fear in his eyes and I asked him if he wanted stronger painkillers. I spoke to the nurse who was unsure because he'd not asked for any help before now. I was incredibly firm with her, explaining that my grandad is a strong, brave and proud man, if he is asking for help it must be bad. She was initially defiant quoting the rules and I insisted, held my ground as I always would for someone I love. Eventually at 6pm she agreed he could have morphine.

She left and for a while I put my faith in her. I tried to call my aunt to get her back to see her dad but I couldn't get hold of her. My grandad was in so much pain I could hear the gargling of his chest, he could hardly breathe. The look of pain and fear in his eyes was horrific. To see a man who had always appeared so strong look at me in total desperation is a moment I will never forget, he was begging me with his look to help him.

My gran was really struggling with everything and the carers who had been coming in for weeks were so concerned for him they decided to stay with me and my gran. He was looking to my gran for comfort and assurance while his breathing got worse. She was telling me I was too young to be there and see this but I knew I was there for a reason.

"It's ok, I am here for a reason. I am here to give you strength because grandad needs YOU," I told her. I sent all my energy and focus to my gran while holding my grandad's hand. I guided her to just help him keep breathing. When my gran said she couldn't do it and went to leave the room I told her calmly she had no choice, he needed her and she had to stay. I promised to keep helping her and she was able to stay. The carers asked me if I wanted to break my grandad's wishes and send him to hospital because they couldn't help and they couldn't get the nurse to come back sooner, she kept saying we were next on the list but it was now nearly 8.30pm and neither her nor my aunt were back.

It was one of the hardest decisions to continue seeing my grandad in that much pain but I knew his wish was to die at home so we kept him home. Each minute of looking into his or my gran's eyes felt like an eternity. Remaining calm, strong, focused and sending all of my energy to them both was a lesson in suspending my feelings for the love of another.

When my aunt arrived she burst into the room, shooed my gran off the bed and proceeded to tell my grandad off. I couldn't believe what I was seeing. The nurse arrived a short while after and finally began to put the morphine driver up. Once it was up, my grandad never spoke again. It took him another nine days to be ready to leave his body but I know that night was his last night conscious and I am honoured to have been there by his side every breath of the way. I know that he felt my support, my strength and my love. I know that my grandparents needed me that night and I was able to be there for them in the way they needed at that time.

Over the next few days, my aunt and I barely left. We tried to re-patch our family for his sake and I promised my grandad I would look after my gran and try to bring my aunt, mum and I back together. I did try, Grandad, but I am sorry that was the wrong promise because you see I asked them for help and they shunned me.

My promise to my grandad now is to learn to have the strength to ask for and receive help.

Following his passing I wasn't told stories of what a great father and husband he was. No I was told all the flaws my grandad had, stories I never wanted nor needed to hear. I know with my hand on my heart that my grandad did his very best for me. As a child he was the one who used to take me to the ice cream parlour when my gran, mum and aunt were having yet another of their vile arguments. He was the one who taught me enough self-defence that I felt safe walking down the street.

He was also the one who taught me not to ask for help.

I love you, Grandad, and I was blessed to have you in my world, you were a true gentleman and I know you did your best to try to protect me. I hope you will be proud that I have learnt that true strength doesn't come from pretending everything is OK; it comes from accepting when it isn't, being vulnerable and asking for help. Darn it, demanding help like I did for you.

I am still not a natural at asking for help, as my closest friends often remind me, but I do now know that strength doesn't come from pretending you're ok.

Strength is admitting you need help and making darn sure you get it.

## The Friends we Keep

As a child I was often told by my Great Granny Merrick that I would
be judged by the company I kept. Loosely meaning, be friends with
the good kids. I fundamentally do not like this or subscribe to this
mantra.

My ability to speak openly about my mother's behaviour has always
seemed to open the floodgates for others and almost attract them.
Many times I have gone on to consider these people my friends.
I have noticed that I have often been drawn to friends who also
have toxic families. People whose mothers in particular were cold,
distant, jealous of them, self-centred and not very loving, if at all. I
have been told some horrific things that parents have done to their
children both as children and as adults.

The thing that strikes me about this now that I have taken a huge
step back in my life to create a life that I really want is how this
happens and what effect this has.

When you have a group of friends who have had similar experiences
it can be easier to open up about your own dysfunctional family.
Without a doubt, talking about our experiences is a big part of
healing, learning and moving on. However I have noticed a flaw
in recovery when you have friends who have the same type of
experiences; you normalise it.

Something that would happen time and time again as I was going
through therapy and then talking to friends with similar experiences
is that even if we all agreed it was wrong there was an air of; mine
was worse, others have survived, it could have been worse, it's in
the past now. Also when I looked at totally removing myself from
my toxic family it seemed to freak out some of the friends who

hadn't done this. Almost as if they took my decision to step away as a judgement or reflection upon them and their choice to stay with their toxic family.

For me, this has hampered my growth. Purely because one of the things I have had to work hard on is my ability to trust myself, my inner voice and my inner strength. I have spent almost all of my life looking outside for validation, and receiving this from others who have yet to heal from their own toxic families isn't a great tactic.

Since I have taken a total step back from most aspects of my life and made a focused effort on rebuilding a life that is what I truly want and makes me deeply happy I have learnt even more about friends. I am not very good at making lasting friends. I have always wanted to be a good person, often driven by a desire to be nothing like my mum. In doing this I have often only let people see the best of me, given so much into my friendships and refused to take much back, that I have in essence created toxic relationships.

This is not to say that my friends have been toxic. That is not where I am going with this at all. More that my experience of life up until the age of 37 has been that I have to be practically perfect or I will be torn down. There is no room for error, no room for growth, no room for flaws and I have to give all of me and expect nothing in return. That is what I was taught by my family and then my marriage and this is something I went on to create in my friendships.

I have been told by friends who have watched me when things get hard that I pull back, pull my shutters down as I would call it. They tell me they want to know when things aren't good, that they want to be there. I have had some friends try to be there but struggled to let them in.

The problem lies in learning to allow someone to support you when you have never experienced that. Learning to allow someone to forgive you when you royally fuck up, when you have never experienced that is hard. Learning how to have healthy relationships when you have never experienced that is HARD.

It doesn't happen overnight.

I know that there are many people out there that I have been a bloody good friend to. I know there are people I have stepped up for, stepped in for, cheered for, celebrated with and been their cheerleader. I am sure there are friends who feel abandoned by me in the last few years. There are conversations that were needed which have never taken place. I also know there are people who have tried so hard to be a good friend to me. I know there are people who have worried, cried, fought and tried to be there.

I would go as far as saying I have pushed everyone and almost everything away in the last few years. I had to. I have had to learn to listen to my own voice, my own heart, my own soul and learn what is and what isn't healthy for me.

Being a good person is ever only half of a person. We all have good and bad in us. We are all flawed. We all have demons we need to face. I have not only faced mine but I have taken them for a walk, sat with them and got to know them. I know the very depths of my soul and I am at peace with it all. I am at peace with the parts of me that would stand up for someone I barely know who is being mistreated. What I am not at peace with is my inability to stand up for myself.

I have learnt that I see myself as a second-class citizen of my own life. I have in all of my relationships, friendships included, not called people out when they have been unfair, unkind and unreasonable, and in doing that I have taught them that it is ok to treat me that way. I have created relationships where I am the only one that I allow to give. I have pushed people away who have tried to support me because I do not know how to be loved. I have accepted people who treat me like I am the only one who makes mistakes.

I once said to a friend after one of the most honest arguments I had ever had with anyone that I felt that our friendship had stretched too far. I actually wrote her a card and hand delivered it to her. I said that I think friendships are like elastic bands and that ours had stretched too far. That I didn't want it to stretch so far that it broke and that I hoped that if we let it rest for a while it would bounce back with love.

It took a few years but blow me down did that become the truth. Just as my life became too much for many, when the pain and trauma I was going through tested every ounce of who I was and every relationship around me, this friendship came through. When I look at that friendship now with a bit of distance it hasn't always been healthy, we have both had a lot of therapy and are able to talk about the deep stuff in life. We are both very honest with each other and have the guts to say things that the other may not like. Now I do believe that we have been able to create a healthy friendship built from the honesty of the past.

I am a huge advocate for therapy. That time and space to talk things through with a professional that isn't clouded by the relationship they have with you and their views on your life is something I believe every adult can benefit from. Heck even kids could do well to have half an hour a week where they can talk things over. Finding the right therapist is so important. It was very clear from the way my friendship bounced back that it stemmed from the work we had both done on ourselves.

These friendships which allow each person to have space to heal, time to totally screw up, and yet still come back with fresh eyes and look to get to know each other again, they are rare and, for me, the real meaning of friendship. One thing I know to be true is that I am grateful for everyone I have ever called my friend, whether or not we still talk, if we have grown apart, or if time has shown that we aren't healthy for each other. I am grateful for any friend I have had who has walked part of my path with me. I have gratitude lists from the past six years and friends play a huge part in those, day in and day out.

The beauty of this life that we lead is that friends can show up in the most unusual of places. There is no time limit as to how long we need to know someone before they become our friend. There is no set amount of time we need to spend with them or even if in some cases we even need to meet them face to face at all.

Friends can arrive out of nowhere. They can come back into our lives at the strangest of times. I have recently had a whole group of old school friends reappear in my life. It couldn't have happened at a better time and the laughs that we share are just like when we were teenagers.

There are people who could call me now and I would drop everything for them. I am slowly learning that they too would do the same for me, I just have to allow them to. I have also learnt that real friendship isn't all the laughs, the fun, parties, games. Sure, they are awesome and I used to be the first to arrange these things. Real friendship is deeper than that. It is the pain. It is not judging each other or forcing opinions on each other. It is forgiveness and letting go of each other's mistakes.

Real friendship is the ability to accept all of someone, the awesome and the awful.

I am blessed with some very real friends.

The more I learn to love and accept myself, the more I am able to be a healthy good friend.

# PART 2: DOING THE WORK

## *Cutting out Negative Influences*

Over the last few years I have done an extensive amount of reading around the topic of narcissists, psychopaths, sociopaths, or 'Cluster B personalities' which I believe is the best term. Having a greater understanding of how or why anyone could treat another human being the way I have been treated throughout my life has helped me make greater sense of it all.

I do believe that knowledge is a form of power and when you are facing a reality where almost anyone who's had a significant role in your life has been toxic, you have to begin to question why this happens. My first theory was that I subconsciously looked for the same kind of experience I grew up with, and this does have some level of basis in common psychological theory.

However, alongside all of the reading I have been on a spiritual awakening in recent years. Unsurprisingly I was brought up to be religious, church on a Sunday, C of E School for primary and secondary and even begging to be confirmed at only 11... anything to please my mother. For a long time I have seen the hypocrisy of people who claim to be religious but treat others terribly. Part of my spiritual awakening has been the realisation that I chose this life before I was born.

I chose my parents, both my daughters chose me and their dad. Go with me on this for a little while as I realise that for some of you this might be quite a deep or out there concept. I believe we are souls living a human experience and part of that experience is the chance to learn lessons. Before we are born we choose the lessons we wish to learn, so those of us that are having a rough old ride down here on earth, we are actually the ones who are learning the most and evolving... as long as we learn the lessons rather than keep repeating them.

Once I was able to grasp this I was able to see that everything we were going through was an awesome opportunity to learn and to grow. One of the biggest lessons I had to learn was that I had the freedom of choice. I choose who I share my precious time and energy with. Having lost every penny of the money that I once had, my home, car and lifestyle, I have been able to see that material things and money can be regained but our energy is incredibly special.

It became extremely important to me that I checked who I spent my time and energy with. This also includes the energy used in thinking about someone... who else has wasted days, weeks or even months overanalysing a situation, person or circumstance?

Over the last three years I have either cut out or removed myself from the majority of people I used to spend time with. The most important but also the hardest have been my mother, grandmother and aunt.

All three of them have at various times shown that they have no love, respect or compassion for me. In fact the last time I saw them I was very close to ending my own life and they more than couldn't have cared less, in fact they chose to belittle me further. Those four minutes have gone on to be the biggest gift they could have given me. For whenever I feel like caving and going back, calling them, checking on them I remember that they were happy to leave me for dead. "Come back now if you really need help. It's Sink or swim" were the words they so kindly used to a woman contemplating driving in front of a bus.

Each of them have their own toxic ways which I am very grateful to be away from now.

By far and away the best book for facing the realities of such relationships and how to identify them, recover and protect yourself in the future is, *The Empathy Trap - Understanding Antisocial Personalities,* by Dr Jane McGregor and Tim McGregor. This book explains how the sociopath operates and how they use apaths to support them.

It helped me see that I am very much an empath. Knowing this has helped me to focus on ways I can find positives from this. There is a test within the book that appeals to my need for proof that I am ok. The inner chatter I have been learning to quieten, and which I explain in another chapter, is key here.

The book talks about gaslighting - which is the systematic attempt by one person to erode another person's reality. You are told false information in such a way that it is designed to make you doubt your own memory. It is a horrible form of psychological abuse and very common part of dealing with any Cluster Bs. Once you are able to see what has happened to you it is vastly easier to accept it and move on.

Within this book I also learnt about apaths. They are the people who turn a blind eye to the actions of the Cluster B. They often end up doing their dirty work for them or they side with the Cluster B to make their case stronger. If you have had any form of Cluster B in your life then you can guarantee that you also have apaths.

When I did a bit of an audit of my life and those around me it transpired that I had found myself around many people who fell into the Cluster B or apathy category. As much as apaths aren't knowingly trying to do harm they are just as harmful to your world as any Cluster B.

The basic test for anyone who is to remain in my life is: do they fill me up or drain me? Will Smith does a brilliant little video about people who fan your flames or douse your fire. Not everyone deserves to be around you! You are so very precious, your life, your energy, your soul has purpose and even if you have to totally rebuild your whole circle, do not give your energy to those who piss on your fire!

It can be so very easy to fall back into the trap of going back to what you know. It is scary to go it alone for a while. But every single person you share your energy with is getting a part of you that you can never get back; that is the single biggest gift you can give to anyone or anything.

I found it quite amazing just how many people I had previously held in high regard that when I actually questioned how I felt around them I realised they also displayed characteristics of the Cluster B and the apath. Maybe because I had become so used to this that I partly created it in others?

If I choose to spend any time with you, I appreciate you wholeheartedly. A large part of my journey has been to get to know myself again and fully which has meant a lot of time alone also. This path has been mine alone to walk and anyone who makes it out the other side with me I am deeply grateful for.

It is not easy to cut the negative influences out of your life. Far from easy but it is essential. Even if it means being or feeling alone for a while this was the most significant part of my journey. Society tells us that blood is thicker than water which is true and even more so when that blood is like poison to you, it is like extra strength poison and therefore even more important that you step away and find yourself.

## Giving up Perfect

For the longest time I was scared to ever put a foot wrong. I was scared of being judged. shamed, picked apart for getting something - anything - wrong.

I put myself under so much pressure to be the perfect mum, wife, student. My belief that I had to be perfect meant that I lost all sight of what it was to be real - to be perfectly imperfect and to connect with people based on my screw-ups. I have since learnt that people do not want the very best of me all the time, that hiding my mistakes and trying so hard only made me feel like shit and made others feel inadequate.

Yes there are those that live their lives waiting to judge and condemn others. Those who always have an opinion on how you or someone else 'should' do things. Yes there are those who don't cheer so loud when you do win, who will minimise it or dim your light but they are not the people needed. I had to learn the very hard way that those who were so quick to pick at my flaws, tell me how they would have (and I should have) done it differently are not my people. In fact I had at one point attracted so many of these people around me that nothing I did was ever good enough.

It didn't matter how hard I worked, what great things I did with and for my daughters, how many times I sorted things out for friends, or helped others improve their lives, they would be silent. When I dared ask for help they would be 'busy', tell me I was strong and didn't need it. Then when I did screw up they couldn't wait to magnify the whole situation. There was at no point any help, support, compassion, kindness or even basic humanity. It was pure condemnation.

This is not real. We all make mistakes. There is not a human being walking this earth who hasn't hurt someone, done the wrong thing, flipped out or got it wrong at some point in their lives. The biggest difference between those who have healed and those who haven't faced their own demons is how quickly they point out your failure and criticise you for it. To focus on only the worst of anyone and ignore all the times that they have supported you, others, been kind and forgiving is not a shame on the person being shamed, it is a sign of how far the person or people judging have to go.

I have learnt the hardest way that being vulnerable is not a weakness it is pure strength. That in my moments of vulnerability where I am brave enough to share the worst moments of my life I do not open myself to the judgement of others but I give them the chance to show me exactly who they are.

Am I proud of the fact that on Christmas Eve 2014 I lost my temper and hurt my own daughter causing a bump and bruise to her head? Hell, no.

Do I own that I did it? Have I always at every stage taken total responsibility for allowing myself to get to that stage in my life? Hell, yes.

I have spent so many long hours questioning every moment that led up to that moment and the biggest reason I have found is this: I stressed myself out trying so hard to be perfect. Even on that day with my leg in an air cast boot, I was the friend that arranged for a magical Christmas elf to come to the house. I was the one who hosted everyone. I was the one in pain and incapacitated but still trying to make the world magical.

It was too much. I needed to be asking for help not trying to keep things perfect, they weren't perfect; I was in pain every day.

I had been brought up to believe that no one would ever help me and I had to be perfect or I would be judged and shamed, which in reality is exactly what happened. None of it would have happened if I had thought more of myself and asked for more help from the moment I injured my ankle alone at Center Parcs with my daughters. Even then I drove us home. My belief that you need to be perfect was my greatest downfall. It hurt my daughters and it destroyed my life.

I am not perfect. At my worst I have hurt those I love the most.

I did not need to be judged. I needed to be supported, cared for, shown compassion, kindness and taught that it is OK to need help. It is OK to ask for help. My greatest gift from all this is that I have learnt that I am far from perfect. I am a massive work in progress and yes, I screwed up in the highest order, but this doesn't mean that moment is all of me. Very far from it. That moment is me when I snapped and I know, and have always known, I will never get there again.

In the most roundabout way it has become a gift.

In that moment and all that followed I had times of thinking the absolute worst of myself but that isn't the case. I had times of questioning if all I knew about myself was wrong. Was I some awful horrible person? No is the conclusion I have come to from most likely an unhealthy amount of soul searching. I am imperfect but I am healing.

My childhood was awful and my mum blamed me for everything, so my marriage was much the same. I knew he was a gambler but I foolishly thought I could save him and he too blamed me for it all. I was not to blame for anything either of them did to me and they aren't to blame for my actions.

I could have healed my imperfect self sooner. I could have faced up to the pain of having my mother ignore me most of the time rather than snapping at my girls after she made me feel like shit. I could have put in stronger boundaries with my ex-husband rather than allowing him to keep pushing my buttons.

Most importantly I could have created a group of people around me where I felt ok to tell them I was hurting and needed help. I could have stopped trying to be perfect.

Trying so hard all the time caused me to snap. I snapped in the worst way imaginable.

The path to forgiving myself for that has been long and hard. The path to learning that there is a middle ground. I don't have to be perfect or a failure. I don't have to have it all together or be broken. I can be and I am a work in progress who is healing each day.

In the middle of this my girls have watched me and learnt. I am beyond blessed to have such an incredible bond with my daughters. For the longest time I thought this was luck because I was told so much different to our reality. The reality is that every time I was there for them when they were sick, told them it was ok when they screwed up, showed them they could calm down after losing their temper and be forgiven, each time I took them to somewhere magical, all of the thousands of times I had done good with them was remembered too. The moment where I snapped and couldn't take it back they didn't hold this above all else.

My children are kind, forgiving and compassionate. I have seen this in them not just with me but in the way they treat other children. While I take responsibility for the worst I have brought into their lives I also take responsibility for the good. Because while I am not perfect I am still a good, kind, forgiving, compassionate person. I am now and I always was. Maybe this is why I struggled so much to find that this doesn't exist in everyone.

Now when I need help I ask for it. Now when things aren't going great I get on with it and don't feel the need to put on a fake smile. Now I have the confidence to go on social media not just saying how positive things are but also when things are tough. I am confident to say that I just cried myself to sleep or stopped believing in myself.

I am not perfect and nor do I need to be.

I have learnt that my strength doesn't come from my positivity. I would actually go as far as to say that pretending to be positive when things are shit is not only weak but also destructive, it certainly led to me destroying my life. True strength is the ability to be vulnerable. To share your losses and your screw-ups, to ask for help, to look for help, to demand help if you need to. To refuse to give in to shame.

Standing up and owning the very worst of me is where my power lies. Judgement is cheap. Compassion and understanding is strength. I hope and I pray that me being honest about how I came to snap like that will help some other mum, dad, aunt, uncle, nanny or grandad ask for help before they try to be perfect.

Do I wish that I could turn back the clock and change that moment. Sure as heck I do but that is not possible. All I can do is work from where I am now, stop beating myself up over it. Stop worrying about what others think and remember that I am not the worst of me. All of the good things didn't disappear in that moment.

I am lucky my girls and I have a very deep bond. We love and respect each other. I am able to be honest with them about how I got to that point, by not asking for help, by trying too hard and I hope that they will learn from my lessons.

Being self-aware enough to face the shittiest parts of who we are and take total responsibility for them and ownership of them is hard. It is easy to blame others and to a point, yes, it is my childhood that got me to this point but it is my responsibility to change that. Blaming, feeling bitter doesn't make any of it better. Learning the lessons, taking them forward to create something more. Building a family who know it's ok to be angry. Your anger is real and it is ok, just don't take it out on others. Saying, "I forgive you" and meaning it. For being understanding to each other when we make mistakes rather than condemning each other. Bringing my girls up to know they can ask me for help at any time and I will drop everything for them, that they are never alone. Knowing that I will never judge them and they can tell me anything, be anything, do anything and I will always support them.

I hope that I am showing them that they are worth more than their mistakes. That you can recover from anything. That they do not ever need to be perfect. I love them no matter what.

I have given up perfect and taken up being real.

## *Finding your own Inner Voice*

For most of my life I have had an inner self-talk that has been little short of degrading. I have been my own biggest critic for as long as I could remember. I caught myself saying a few years ago that I would never talk to anyone else the way that I talk to myself.

I drop something and my head says, "What they hell are you doing? You're so stupid, can't you even carry properly?"

If I eat something unhealthy, it's a torrent of putdowns, guilt trips and shaming myself.

When there is a big opportunity available I will go for it despite the whole chatter in my head telling me how awful I am, and how I won't be able to/can't do it.

Before a date I always think they will be disappointed when they see me because I'm too fat, talk too much, talk too fast, on and on and on the list of internal putdowns go.

When I took the time to question where this negativity came from, who it actually was saying these things to me, I realised it came from those people who had gaslighted me over the years. They had brainwashed my inner chatter. Even though they were not around anymore, they had in effect taken over my inner voice. Even with no contact they were still having a huge internal impact upon me.

While I did a lot of work to overcome this negative self-talk chatter and the constant putdowns, and was able to go on to achieve quite a lot, it was not until I found my own inner voice that I was able to silence them and take back my power.

Your own inner voice will never put you down. It will never call you names, belittle you. Your inner voice comes from your higher self and your connection to everything you are capable of doing and being, which is totally limitless. You came to this earth to shine. Your inner voice is your inner cheerleader, if you will. You need to connect with it and nurture it.

Do you have an inner cheerleader?

If you don't then this needs to become your number one priority.

Without your own inner voice being your champion there is nothing that anyone else can say to you or see in you that will get you to believe how truly special and unique you are. You can watch as many motivational videos as you like. You can attend all the self-help and personal development seminars in all the world. No one can do this for you but you.

How do you find that voice? You begin by looking for it.

An independent visualisation that I find helpful is to picture a classroom full of loud chattery children. Be in that room, there can be as many loud children as you wish but these will be your current self-talk. They are all arguing, aggressive, laughing and joking, but right at the back of the class is a meek and timid child talking very quietly. You focus all of your attention on the quiet child, they may even look a little like you did as a child. Walk towards them and focus only on them. Dim out everything else and listen intently upon their voice. They are the representation of your inner voice.

You will need to practice connecting in to your inner voice and quietening down the negative self-talk.

You may be incredibly good at this and find it easy to listen to your own inner voice. If that is your reality I am incredibly happy for you.

I found that having spent my whole life with this inner critic that I often still have to quieten it. I have to keep training my mind to go in search of my inner truth and focus on that instead. I am not always successful, sometimes an old toxic behaviour comes back and I give in. Then under that influence I also begin to listen to how useless, ugly, unworthy, warped, unwanted, waste of space I am, and for a time I still can give in. After all, I am only human. I am not perfect and nor do I need to be.

The key to remember here is that every day, hour or minute I have the choice to go inward and go in search of my own inner voice again. One thing I can assure you is it will never berate you, chastise you or belittle you for losing your path.

Your inner voice knows how awesome you are and will always remind you of that. Find it, focus on it and nourish it.

## Facing your Shadow

Your shadow (or shadow self) is all of the parts of you that you aren't proud of. The parts which most of us conceal. Carl Jung said that, "The shadow is an instinctive and irrational part of us that is prone to psychological projection, in which a perceived personal inferiority is recognised as a perceived moral deficiency in someone else." This means that the flaws you see in others are a reflection of the areas where you believe yourself to be lacking. Carl Jung is a highly respected psychologist and the theory of projection is often spoken about, however if you are able to face the darker parts of your personality then you will lessen this.

Projection can also happen in a positive stance and I know I have done this throughout my life and projected lots of amazing qualities on to others. When someone is treating you horrifically you make excuses for them: "they had a hard childhood", "they are overcoming addiction", "they are mentally ill". Poor behaviour and treatment of others needs boundaries and to be called out. Period.

I am not totally on board with Carl Jung's description of our shadow self. When I look at working with our shadow self I am thinking of the things that if you could take back you would. The things that you are least proud of and would happily push to the very back of your mind. The most important thing to remember when doing shadow work is that we all have dark and light within us and that being in touch with the dark makes our light shine brighter. The old saying used to be having skeletons in your closet - this is opening your closet and having a chat with those skeletons and getting to know them.

I find meditation a great tool to use when working with the parts of ourselves that we have kept hidden for many reasons. It helps us become more relaxed and open to the parts of us that have been hidden. When going into shadow work it is essential that you frame this with yourself that we ALL have dark and light. What has been done is passed and cannot be changed and there is no shame to be had in whatever you find. We are all entitled to make mistakes and this is part of your journey. Everyone is entitled to learn from their mistakes.

Write a list of all the things you are not proud of in your life. Give yourself a minute to sit with each one, think what you might have learnt from that. What triggered you to take that action at the time, would you do the same again?

If there is a person involved in each of these do you need to speak to them about it or if speaking to them is no longer an option because maybe they are someone you have needed to let go of, then writing them a letter (that you never post) can be a very powerful way to connect and let go of this experience.

Here you are looking to forgive yourself. Not to blame others for your actions. Not to look for them to forgive you but for you to forgive yourself. Nothing can be gained by you feeling shame for anything you have done in your past. Shame, guilt, fear, these are all very low levels of consciousness. You are not serving yourself by remaining in this state.

Learning to forgive yourself is a freeing skill.

This might take many attempts at being able to sit with each part of your shadow. I found that it took about a year of this kind of work on and off. It did lead me to a dark place, I ended up feeling rather depressed and alone, so I would encourage you to get those you trust to be your safety net during this time and keep an eye on you.

This could also be a good time to consider a good therapist, particularly, someone who understands shadow work. Don't be afraid to ask if they know this concept.

If you can go through these things alone that is great, and remember you don't have to tell anyone what you're doing if you don't want to. It was easier for me, however, to be open about the worst of me because that meant it had less power over me.

## *You are Worthy*

There is not a soul on this earth who is not worthy of healing and love.

From those who have been tortured by others to those who have done the torturing. In every given moment on this earth we all have the ability to decide who we are and what we want to be.

We have all done things which aren't kind, compassionate... this is what makes us human.

So whatever the story is that you have been telling yourself it is time to learn that you are worthy.

Your heart beats for a reason. You were brought to this earth with a gift and a place. You are totally worthy of the feelings of joy and peace, and to know that things can and will come together for you.

My personal story all stems from a core belief that I was not worthy.

When I look back at some of the incredible opportunities I have had, the coaches I have been blessed to work with, often as a gift from them to me, I know there have been so many chances for me to shine incredibly brightly. I have been given chances many have not, chances some can only dream of.

What held me back each time? I thought I was horrendous, a waste of space, unloved, unlovable and mostly unworthy of anything good.

Of course for the most part this wasn't what I wanted to believe so I set about trying to convince myself of my worth. I learnt about the Law of Attraction, I said affirmations, I worked with an energy coach. But nobody, not the psychotherapist, counsellor, energy coach, business coach, mentor, or the university lecturer who believed in me in a way no one else ever has in my life, no one could believe in me until I believed in myself.

I had to decide that I AM worthy. I am worthy of all the wonderful things that life has to offer. No one could tell me that, take me through some tool or path. I had to sit with my own shit and decide it didn't define me. That no matter who I was born to, what anyone else thought of me, good or bad, I am worthy.

I am worthy and so are you.

The moment I realised I am worthy was a moment of clarity. This was a path I had to walk alone. A path that led me to the darkest moments. I let go of everything and almost everyone on my path to realising that I am worthy.

I don't have to beg for anyone's attention. I don't have to meet anyone else's idea of good, bad or anything else. I am worthy. Just as I am.

No matter where you are on your journey, I promise you; YOU ARE WORTHY.

## *Learning to Nothing Them*

When you have lived through feeling like someone has set out to destroy you it is natural and normal to hate them. It is natural to want to blame them for all the things that happen around that time. It can be easy to become the victim, well in all fairness, you are the victim.

Here is the harsh truth, though. In being the victim, in allowing yourself to continue in this role and send energy to them, still you are still allowing them the power.

If I could calculate the amount of my life in analysing, over-analysing, reliving, wondering how I could have changed things in the way that I had dealt with my mum, ex-husband and the family court, it would be months of my life.

There are so many reasons why this isn't healthy.

When we think about traumatic situations again and again we send energy to it. This creates a link to it that is literally feeding that negativity. We are creating an energetic cord with that person and situation. We are tethering ourselves to that experience and person.

When we go over these things and think about the people we have been hurt by we reactivate that pain. We reconnect ourselves with it and keep that cycle alive. The more we speak about it the more we feed it. Some amount of reflection is needed, but with the clear focus of learning the lessons and letting go. This is not a simple path but letting go is essential to healing.

The next step once the lessons have been learnt is to learn to nothing these people.

It sounds so simple but it is not, well it might be for you but it sure as heck wasn't for me.

When I say 'nothing' them I mean stop blaming, stop thinking and overthinking about them. A massive one for me was to stop adding meaning to the things they say and do. It is totally possible to not see or speak to someone but to be energetically still linked to them and to still be allowing them to dominate a huge part of your thoughts, energy and life.

I found that I owed it to myself to take back this time, energy, space and focus.

I am going to share with you the many ways I have worked to release myself from the past. Some of them may work for you and some you might find a bit too much. Please only ever do what you feel comfortable with, after all, you are the expert of you.

## *The Pomodoro technique*

**Write letter under time restrictions -**

ᵤₑₜ ₑr for a reasonable amount of time, say 40 minutes.

a. Turn off your phone off, emails, any distractions and tell family and friends to leave you in peace... if you have a busy life and a few people to deal with, a little trip away might be needed.

b. Get yourself grounded and centred in whatever way you choose.

c. Get some loose paper and a pen that feels comfortable.

d. Begin the timer and write.

e. Write everything you have ever wanted to say to them, let it flow straight out of you without filter or judgement.

f. Spelling and neatness don't matter, you don't even have to write in clear English, just get it all out of you.

g. If you cry let the tears fall, if you get angry channel that into your writing, let it all out, feel whatever you need to feel and let them know about it.

h. When the alarm goes - stop.

i. Stop right where you are.

j. If you need to write a letter to someone else, and you feel able to, move on to the next person and repeat steps a-j.

k. When you are done, take the letters to a safe place and burn them.

l. Let it all go to the universe.

m. Take a moment to appreciate what you have done.

n. Allow yourself time to rest, recharge and recover after this as it can be a very emotional task.

o.  Keep your fluids up and eat light and healthy after, don't drink alcohol or eat fatty foods.

**2.    Therapy**

Finding that space to talk to someone is a huge step in recovery. I know that for me I had to explore so much. In hindsight I wish I had picked someone who had experience of working with Cluster B personality abuse because that would have been even more effective but I am still very grateful for my weekly sessions. That 1-2-1 time is invaluable. However, I do not think therapy alone can do it. I also believe there are things we need to do for ourselves.

**3.    Energetic Cord Cutting**

When we think about someone in any way we are creating an energetic bond or cord with them. These cords are a bit like tubes and energy can flow both ways. When we are linked with people we love and care about the energy is usually, but not always, positive. In fact any cords can be draining, as even those who wish us no harm can drain our energy if we allow them to, and that is not healthy for them or us.

Keeping our own energy in a high vibration is not only good for us but also for everyone around us. It is a bit like energetic housekeeping.

The most basic way of cutting cords is to ask for the help and guidance of Archangel Michael and his sword of blue flame to cut all cords that do not serve you and bind them with light.

This is a basic energy 101 that we would all benefit from doing each day and night.

However if you have a long standing connection with someone who is negative it could be beneficial to seek some energy healing. I have had pranic healing and 1-2-1 energy coaching where psychic attack from a person I had barely seen in years was discovered.

Much like when we overthink the past or when we create energetic cords with people, if there is someone who is consistently sending us bad thoughts and feelings it can tether with us. Clearing this down is healthy for you and for them. After all, anyone wishing harm on another is not in a good place themselves and needs that energy back.

I also use a meditation about four times a week to keep my cords clear.

### 4.    The freezer technique

I love the freezer technique and have seen it make dramatic changes in my life. It is so simple and powerful.

When you keep thinking about someone or they keep popping into your mind or life when you no longer want them to, this is a simple and effective way to kindly let them go.

You take a piece of paper. Write their name on it. Then think of the most kind, loving and caring thing you can possibly think about them. The first time this could be a bit of a challenge but it is an important step in this process, you must send them good vibes.

Then you take a yellow pen or highlighter and while drawing a circle around them three times say, "I bind you with light". So three circles and three times saying, "I bind you with light".

You then put it in the freezer. You can put it in a bag of water if they need to be frozen from your life more, or if you have had a particularly bad experience with them and would like them to have a taste of their own medicine, purely so they can learn from it then there is another option.

Now if you take the final step it is vitally important that you are in a good space yourself as anything you send into the universe will come back to you. If you take this step before you are able to wish well on someone then it will not bode well for you.

You can put their binded with light name into a lemon and then freeze the lemon.

The key with all of this is that you find it in your heart and soul to only send them good wishes. You never need to let them into your life and world again but don't stoop to the level of wishing any harm.

5.    I do not know - let it go - send them love

As an empath I often know what others are feeling. I am not, however, a mind reader and no matter what I think, I do not know what someone else's intentions are. Learning and accepting this is a huge part of moving on from someone, not hating them and achieving the nothing that brings freedom.

I must admit to, at times, thinking that things that have been done or said to me, around me or about me have a meaning. I assume that I know why someone did something.

This is total bollocks.

I do not know, and nor do you, why someone has done the things they do. We often don't even know the root cause of why we do some of our strangest and silliest actions.

It could even be that those who we see as having harmed us were contracted to teach us these lessons and they signed up to help us learn. Who knows? One thing I know for sure is that when we apply a meaning to the actions of others we add energy and power to it.

When we have gone to the lengths of removing or drastically limiting someone's involvement in our lives to the bare minimum, but still say we know why they are doing things, we are deluding ourselves. Not only are we deluding ourselves, adding power to it but we are also recording with it. None of this matches the desired outcome.

While it is natural for someone to pop into your head, I have a simple way of stopping this from then derailing your mind into becoming focused, once again, on them and the past, and all the coulda, shoulda, wouldas. When something pops into your mind, remind yourself, "I do NOT know" what they, think, what they are doing, etc. Let the thought go, I have to imagine it drifting off in a balloon and then send that person love.

If you can get to the point where the second you think of them, you're going: "I do not know" - let it go - send them love, then you are free from them.

Then you finally nothing them.

It takes time, it won't happen overnight but the more and more you train your brain the more and more it will instinctively do it.

Learning to nothing them is a process. Keep taking steps and one day it will just arrive.

## My Value

I had no idea of my value for the longest time.

I know I didn't know it because of the way I allowed others to treat me, the way I disrespected myself and the total fear I had of charging when I set up my businesses.

I kept looking outside of myself to the world around me for markers of what my value was. I was very quick to accept negative feedback and incredibly slow to take on anything positive. It didn't matter what I achieved; a degree during awful life circumstances and packing out events and being told they had saved lives. I always accepted the voice which told me the negative as correct.

Many people who met me over the years told me I seemed confident. Some even had the gall to tell me I had to be pushed down a bit to keep my feet on the ground. The thing is, in the quiet of my mind, I wasn't replaying all the people who said amazing things to me and about me. No, I was replaying every negative thing.

Each time I stepped through my fear and did something that was a bit out there I was hypervigilant for any negative feedback. I was looking out for the people to say you're not good enough, who do you think you are doing this?

Was it any surprise that I always found them?

It didn't matter how many people were thanking me. How many were telling me I had a gift. No, all that I heard were those negative remarks.

Why?

Because I didn't value myself.

No one can be right for everyone. Not even pizza is liked by everyone and I sure as heck am not pizza.

My value isn't to connect with the whole world. I see that now. My value isn't to have other people who have stood on stages and told their story to get it and to praise me. My value is in being raw, real, vulnerable and trusting that out there in this huge world there is someone who needs to hear my story. That somewhere there is someone else who never feels good enough, no matter how thin they get, how many people they help, how many friends they make, they still feel like they are worthless.

My value lies in the fact that no matter how close I came, I have never given up. That no matter how dark my days and nights have been at times I have always put my awesome daughters first.

My value lies in the fact that I really care about everyone who comes into my life. Sometimes more than I bother to care for myself. That I would and have given my last £1 to someone else before now and most likely would do it again.

My value is in the fact that I have finally stopped talking about writing this darn book and decided that no matter what else is going on for me I will find a way to get this out into the world.

At last I can see that there will always be those waiting to judge, criticise and give their opinion on your life no matter what you do. You can hide away from the world and there will still be someone who will find a way to pass judgement.

My value is in knowing that no matter how alone I have ever felt I am not alone. I have never been alone. I know that if I were brave enough there are lots of people I could call and they would help me because somewhere along the line I helped them.

My value is in knowing that by sharing the worst of me, I might just be able to help other people see that they aren't some awful person. That we all make horrible mistakes. That nothing is so dark that you cannot climb your way back out of the hole.

There is no magic potion. There is no secret. No one is going to come and save you.

My value is in the simple fact that I refuse to give in. I refuse to be defined by my mistakes. I am so much more than the times I've lost my temper and flipped my shit. I am the thousands of other times that I could have and maybe should have lost my shit with those who hurt me but I didn't. I am defined more by the fact that I have always taken responsibility for my own life. Even as young as eight when I used to cook for myself or fourteen when I got myself away from my abusive mother.

I am not the moments where I have nearly given in. Yes, they are very much part of my whole. I own my darkness and I own it good. I own that for such a long time I thought that I wasn't worthy of anyone's time or energy so I pushed away offers of help and gave far too much to those who treated me badly.

I own that I knew so little of what it is to be loved, truly deeply, unconditionally that I didn't for a long time know how to love myself or allow myself to be loved. The love that I had been taught wasn't love at all. It was allowing myself to eroded, disrespected, used and emotionally trampled on and becoming little more than a slave.

I own that I have taught myself how to love and be loved.

Learning how our brains work is one thing. Learning the psychology of attachment theory, personality disorders and how to heal from emotional abuse is totally brilliant on an intellectual level. Understanding the theory and putting it into practice to heal are totally different things.

Gaining the strength to own all that is good and all that is bad in my life and cut those who bring no kindness into my world has been hard. The times that I would fall into the trap of wishing they would be different if I called them. If I explained, put boundaries in place. The level to which my family were willing to go is astounding.

Walking my personal path to freedom has been testing. I have spent so long wishing things were different. Wishing my family had any compassion, kindness or genuine care in them at all has cost me months, maybe years, of my life.

Learning I am strong enough to rebuild a life where I do value myself has been tricky. As has learning to value my time, my energy, my focus and my love. The people I choose to spend time with deserve to get the very best I have to offer at that time. They deserve me to have looked after my needs and made sure that we can live a healthy and fulfilling life.

My value is in the fire that is in my heart. The same fire that sparked the strength to get away when I was 14 and again when I was 21, is now ready, at 37, to let it all go. To rebuild everything without those who take but do not give. To rebuild knowing that my girls and I are a blessing and we deserve people in our lives who can see that.

I do love a quote and the one that springs to mind here is, "In the midst of winter, I found there was within me an invincible summer."

My value is my ability to get back up. To keep on creating and learning and doing my best to be the best example I can be to my girls who are now and always have been my whole world.

I hope my value is in the hope I can give to others, that if I can learn and grow from this then you can too.

## *It is not a Competition*

Life is not a competition. No matter how much we have been put into competition mode by the society we live in; it is not a race to the top, nor the bottom for that matter.

Each of us is here on this earth with a unique purpose. That purpose has nothing to do with the wealth we can accumulate or the level of hardship we can endure.

During the worst times of my life I learnt to stop sharing so much of my experience because this was my journey, my lesson to learn. Also I found that most really don't care, they only care to compete and say how hard they or someone they know have had it. That you should just do this, do that, flip a switch and be better.

This isn't because they are unkind. It is how the human brain works. Most people can only understand to their level of experience. So as you speak to them about your own personal tragedy, the majority of people are trying to rationalise it against something they too have experienced. This is not helpful to you. To hear the opinions of people who have no idea what it is like to live through your personal muddy waters is not helpful.

It amazed me the amount of times I was told that barely seeing my children wasn't as bad as having cancer. Then when it came to my mum the amount of people who then needed to tell me about their awful mothers and how much worse they were. Each time I felt myself wanting to scream... it is NOT a competition.

Each of us face our own hardships in life. They are not harder or worse than anyone else's. They are hard to us. It is not a competition and no one, not a single person on this earth has the right to tell you they have it or had it harder than you. They are not swimming through your mud. They have not experienced all the things you have and developed the same perspective.

I found that removing myself from any form of competition gave me freedom. It also freed me from the need for anyone else to understand. While finding others who had been through similar helped me feel less alone, it did not help me face things and move on.

The need for understanding from others is a path that doesn't help through the shittiest past of my life. Accepting that no one can know how it felt for me and that I need to face the darkest parts of my life, is freeing my soul.

For the longest time I just longed for someone to say that they knew and it would be OK. That they got it. That never happened. If ever I mentioned the not-great-stuff in my life, people either went into competition mode about how much harder they had it or they got bored of hearing my crap.

Being realistic about this, do you want to spend the rest of your life hearing other people's trauma and pain? In my experience even the trained, qualified and paid counsellors, therapists, and coaches don't want to swim in your mud with you. They want to be the one to give you a magic solution. Get you to see it positively. To reframe it, to change your perspective. Well one thing I learnt, that didn't help.

What if you and you alone need to get your head, heart and soul around the shit that has happened in your life? What if rather than comparing your hardship with others you need to get away from what is causing it - yes this has to be phase one. Then what if rather than holding it together all the time, trying to find the positive, trying to focus on the good, trying to put my best face forward... what if, all along, what I needed to do was allow myself to break?

What if rather than competing and comparing to be the best, or have survived the worst... what if to be able to truly heal I first needed to fall apart, completely, utterly and totally?

What if I needed to stop being "the strong one" and "the strongest person I know"? What if I needed to give up the strength or the show of being strong, that front I'd created around myself to try to protect myself? What if, all along, I needed to break to let it all go?

You see I am not competing with anyone. Not even myself, as I used to say. I used to say that the only person I was in competition with was the person I was the day before. Well, hell to that. I am not in competition with myself. Not least as that implies that the only progression to be found is upwards and I don't find that to be true.

My gift wasn't found when I was working two businesses, doing a degree, caring for two incredible children single-handed, being sociable and arranging parties for friends. I didn't find my gifts during the times when people said they wondered how I did it all. When I'd meet people and they would say how amazingly positive my social media was. I didn't find it in the days I would get up at 4am to study and work before the school run. I didn't find it in the nights I would study until 2am and still be up singing songs with my girls before school and taking them to their hobbies after. Those days were amazing and fun but I didn't find my heart and soul there.

I found my heart and soul, my power in the time that I fell totally apart. Allowing myself to break for the first time in my life. To stop caring what anyone thought of me. To give up any consideration for those who spend more of their lives judging others than living themselves, in breaking I found my true strength.

I used to say when my mum had a breakdown that I didn't have the luxury of falling apart like that. Thankfully for me I haven't reached that stage. I got to a very different stage but I can see that the day I was ready to end it all was the greatest gift. For no other reason that I knew I'd reached my rock bottom. I couldn't get any lower, any more broken than planning the words for my suicide notes.

I know that I haven't been born into an easy life. My family are quite simply evil. It took me 36 years to see that enough to find the bravery to let go of them and never ever look back.

The trauma of being dragged through family court for years was something I would never wish on another soul. Until you experience the horror of that place and the unbelievable lies that so- called 'professionals' will say on a witness stand, you don't know how intrinsically broken our society is. Finding out that the systems I used to have faith in were so broken was a real moral shock for me and one that I have had to work hard at letting go of wanting to make it better.

For a long time I wanted to take up the banner and fight for a better justice system that truly understands. That looks deeper into things rather than making snap judgements and then fighting for those even if it means lying. But I do not think that is my path, only time will tell.

I am deeply grateful that I was able to take what I learnt and help two other families within the system reach outcomes that were truly in the best interests of the children. That is at the root cause of the biggest issue with the family court system. It puts parents against each other in a vile competition. One where there are only ever losers. The children lose, any parent with a heart can only lose and all that is gained is more money for the solicitors.

Life is not a competition.

Hardships aren't a competition.

Success isn't a competition.

For me, life is about lessons and learning them before they repeat over and over.

My lessons are:

- I am worthy of love.
- Love is not what I was taught as a child, that is abuse. Abuse with "I love you" at the end is not love.
- I do not have to be positive all the time, sometimes life is shit and that is ok.
- I can do this, all of it, the good days, the shitty days, being broke and rebuilding my life.
- My girls loving and respecting me is my biggest achievement.
- Our world depends on me getting my shit together.
- My girls never needed me to be perfect, they need me to show them that no matter what happens they can heal, recover and move on to be happy, healthy and full of FUN!
- This too shall pass, it might pass like a gallstone but it will pass.
- I need to trust my heart, my soul, my light and stop looking to others to save me, heal me, give me the answers - I am my own darn hero!
- I will never, ever give in. My heart beats for a reason and as long as it naturally beats I will be here shining my light, broken, healed or any stage in between.

Giving up the competition allows me to live each day as the total gift that it is. Each day that I open my eyes is a chance to learn more, grow more and experience more. Some days will be awesome and some might be awful but I am not comparing my life to anyone else's. Each day I get up and do the best I can with that day.

Living a life that is free from competition allows me to be truly happy for others when they do well. To not compare when they are going through hardship and to keep out of judgement, I do not have to know or understand someone else's path to be there for them.

A life free from competition allows for a life full of compassion for myself and others.

# PART 3: HEALING

## *Moving Forward*

Moving into my own home was a big step forward. It gave me space to meditate when I felt the need. As an empath who is so connected to the emotions and feelings of others, having this space to clear down emotionally and rebuild was a key step for me.

Yes things still went wrong, or should that be poor choices I had made before kept knocking at my door, but I realised my challenge was to keep moving forward each day in the faith that in time I would be able to find a resolve for everything.

Sitting back and feeling all woe is me, I've had a hard life, my mum is mean, I've got no money left could have been an option. It could also have been an option to start drinking a bottle of wine a night to forget the day job, the last 3½ years and so on. Thankfully I was able to see that such a path wasn't going to get me anywhere except further down the hole I already had to climb my way out of.

Yes, I still wished for miracles each day. Heck if life could go downhill so fast, why on earth couldn't it go up just as fast?! I worked on trying to switch my mindset back to the positive place it had been in when my life was going to the places I wanted it to.

Some days it was great, others I fell back into negative thinking and actions. Some days were so rubbish I had to give in and go back to bed!

At first, all I promised myself is that I would do the day job, try to keep happy and pay all of my current bills, one at a time. I would, at no point, call in sick to work or miss time with my girls.

After the particularly awful day I told you about in 'Hold the Fuck On!' I realised that the time for excuses had passed. I needed to move my life forward at a much greater pace than I had been doing recently. The way I see it, I had two choices: moan about my day job, lack of money, tiny flat and no car OR I could get on with something I had in front of me for ages. I had taken on a book-writing course about two years before but never got anywhere with it.

I also wasn't happy with my weight and health so I committed to getting active each and every day. Whether it was a walk, jog or trip to the gym that came with my job... I'd had free gym membership for almost six months and been about five times. That is not good enough. I was and am in charge of my life as it is right here and right now. Each choice that I make builds the life that I have in the future.

There is a time of healing where you need to face the demons and then there is a time where you need to get on with moving forward again. Each step does not have to be huge but each day does need to have some action in it that will move things in the right direction.

When things have been static or stagnant for too long, as I had allowed my life to become, it can seem to be a daunting task to get moving again. Making it about small daily tasks that are easy to achieve allows for lots of mini wins. I found at times that the wins were as small as contacting a friend each week to ask how they are. To eating healthily that day. Taking the exercise.

Each tiny win is a mini success and needs to be celebrated.

Within less than a month my life felt so much different. The tiny steps so added up to big moves forwards. This book that had been talked about, thought about, dreamed about was completed, being edited and conversations with publishers were being had within weeks. Life can change quickly. All it takes is that forward movement to get some momentum going and a little faith in the universe and magic.

Creating that allows the universe to meet us halfway and create with us.

### Remembering Good Times

When life seems to be handing out one harsh experience after another it can be easy to forget what it was like when life was good. Trauma has a way of impacting our minds and putting such events on a bit of a re-loop. The fear of what is going to go wrong next can be as painful as the experience itself.

I know that after 18 months of feeling like my heart was being shattered into a million pieces once or twice a week as the time with my girls was over; it became hard to do much else other than survive. Moving into survival mode to be able to get through the most awful times of our lives is one of our natural human abilities. What we will do when we are in survival mode is not a reflection of who we are as a person, more our will to keep going against the odds.

I spent most of my childhood in survival mode. Doing what I had to do to get through whatever horrific thing, extreme outburst, months of being ignored would come next. It can become natural to live that way and look for situations that need you to bring out your survivor. But life is not just about survival, it is also about the good times.

Looking for and remembering the good times in life is one of the bridges I used to bring myself out of survival mode and into being ready to thrive again. Getting out the photos of the laughter, the fun and the memories with good, kind, funny people. Connecting the mind with the feelings of joy, watching a movie if needed, putting on a song and having a dance.

What we think about most we create. Learning to focus on the good in our lives and in the world around us cultivates those pathways within us. Yes, writing a daily gratitude list sets us up for the day, and ending the day with gratitude puts everything in context. Meditation allows the mind to calm but I also needed to look for the good.

Something that I found incredibly hard when life seemed to be getting more and more challenging and there was little good stuff, was how boring I found it to talk to people. It's not fun to be the person who is always going through something tough. I decided to shift that up and always find something fun that was happening and share that. It allowed for more fun things to be shared with me also and helped me change my perspective on the world around me. Yes, if I was asked directly about the tougher parts of my life I would answer but in the main I vowed to keep my conversations light and upbeat.

Where focus goes, energy flows.

By making small but consistent steps towards shifting the focus away from the trauma, the past and the current not-great-things, towards the fun, the interesting and the things I liked, I was helping to create more of them. In shifting my daily energy from that of being in the midst of the storm to being positive and expectant for good things to happen I allowed the positive things to arrive.

I try to think of myself as a human magnet when doing this. Whatever energy I am sending out into the universe is what I will be attracting in, so the more positive energy I am able to put out and to share the more can come back to me. If it is a tough day then just chill the energy out, don't pump it out there, allow it to pass. But if it is good then allow it to flow, to connect with others of good energy and create a mutual exchange of the good stuff. This is not about putting on a mask of positivity when life is tough, more about allowing a breather when things feel like they are on a downward spiral.

Even in the worst of days we are able to find a moment for joy. Laughter can be the best medicine during anything we go through and these moments of being able to put down the heavy stuff of our lives gives us the respite we need before going back to face it again.

In remembering the good times we allow ourselves to see that they can come back into our lives again and that the tough stuff will pass.

## When the Punches Just Keep Coming

As a believer in the Law of Attraction - what you feel and think, attracts your life experience - I find it more than a little testing when the punches just don't let up.

Having the belief that 'as within, so without' means we can sometimes do the work to fix the within but the turmoil that we have created previously just keeps on sending its shockwaves.

It is more than a little disconcerting when those who have known you for a long time start to admit you have had the roughest ride of anyone they know. When people stop telling you their problems because they look at you and think, nope, you've got enough of your own.

The worst is when you begin to feel like you are making positive steps forward, that you have begun to get a hold of the almighty shit storm that has become your life and then boom, along comes another round. In these moments where you are suddenly brought back down to your knees this is the time to keep on saying, "this too shall pass" and "I am loved and always have been". Keep moving forward, keep putting one foot in front of the other and tell yourself it can't and won't last forever.

The thing I have found the hardest about the years of things going wrong, more wrong and then worse again is that I got bored of it. I was bored of always being the friend with stuff going wrong. Always having something else that I could totally justifiably moan about. I got sick of being told I was strong. I got sick of holding on. I got tired of holding on. I became tired of trying to find a way to see the good in it all.

If fact in the end I gave up seeing the good in it all and began to accept just how shitty it was. I began to see that it is what it is. Everything that happened was as a result of a choice I had actively or at times passively made before now. There were days that it was too much. Those days were some of the longest I have lived through.

Trying not to slip into the 'poor me' mental state is one of the biggest challenges when things keep on going wrong. The task here is to begin to look for the good everywhere and in everything. There is no more important time in your life to lean into gratitude than when it feels like everything is going wrong. Don't slip in to drama. Yes it is shit. Yes it is hard but it doesn't need to be catastrophised. Freaking out and flipping out doesn't change anything.

I have cried when I have received letters, had a moment of panic when my car was clamped and I had no money on me to even get home, much less go and pick my girls up. Of course, I am human and not a robot but me falling apart wouldn't have changed a darn thing.

Keeping a calm head allows for the possible solutions to be seen. There are always choices that can be made no matter how bad things get. If I could go back to three years ago when things had begun to go bad and taken a bit more responsibility for building a better future things wouldn't have got to where they are. That is a fact.

I am facing the reality of my choice to ignore things previously. Was it totally reasonable that I focused on trying to hold my head and heart together for my kids' sake even though I felt totally broken inside? Hell yes! To the point where if I had to do it all over again I don't actually think I would do things any differently. When life is going wrong it can be so easy to look outside of ourselves and blame.

Blame so many things.

I know I have lived through things which are unthinkably unfair, unjust, unkind and uncalled for.

My question to myself has had to be, what am I learning from this? My question has to be, what can I take from this to build a better future? Not poor me, I am so hard done by. No matter who tells me that I don't deserve many of the things that happened, and I am totally sure my girls didn't deserve it either, if I can face this and look for the lesson, stand up and take those punches and refuse to be knocked out, eventually in time I will win.

There is no punch that is so hard that it can knock you out of the game entirely, unless you choose to give in. I have come so close to that choice, so close it no longer bears thinking about but in that moment where I had chosen to give in something inside me was and is stronger and I came back fighting.

I do believe that we all have an inner spark, an inner fighter and it kicks in at a different stage in life for each of us. Mine needed to see me go to the 12th and final round before I began to fight back. When those punches keep on coming we have to fight back. Whatever fighting back means at that time. For me fighting back has been getting up each day and writing. Writing while holding down a job. While looking after my awesome girls and dealing with the guilt of having next to no money and living in a tiny rented flat. Writing while walking everywhere because I no longer have a car.

For the longest time I just kept taking the punches. I just kept accepting all that life had to throw at me. Accepting that I had made some bad and some awful decisions. Well, in the fight of life, that isn't enough. Sometimes, no matter what you feel like you deserve you have to get back up and get back in the game and begin to start throwing some punches too.

Allowing myself to be punished by life has been my choice. I have chosen to let things go down as far as they have and it is my responsibility to rebuild from the hole that I have created. The thing that I am able to see today versus the days where I felt like giving up is that today I now see that I haven't built a hole in my life, I have cleared out all of the junk from my life. I have invested the time and energy into facing my past and clearing out junk that gave me such unsteady foundations. I have cleared out my physical life from almost all possessions that have any connection to the past. I have cleared out my heart from any connections to the past by working to let them go. I have cleared my mind of the duff programmes that other people had tried to place in there. I have had the bravery to sit down with my soul, the wonderful bright shiny parts and the dark, nasty, spiteful and shameful parts and been able to make my peace with both.

Each one of those punches I have received from life I have needed. I have needed them to show me just how much fight I do have in me. I am so deeply grateful for every single challenge that I have faced and I do take responsibility for every single one of them. I did create this. Every time I felt sorry for myself, I didn't appreciate the life that I had when it was going well. Every time I felt like I had it worse than others, I created this life where I got to realise that I am not living a harder life than anyone else. I am living the life that I created.

As much as I have created this three years, eight months, three weeks and six days of almost relentless punches I have previously created lots of joy, fun, happiness, laughter and a fair amount of magic. When I created all of that before, I was still in the shadow of my past. Now I am free from it and I am free to create the future that my girls and I deserve.

Each punch has brought be a valuable lesson, I am so very grateful for each of them. I have learnt more, forgiven more and let go of more than I ever imagined possible. I am ready to stand back up, take hold of those punches and get back into swinging into life again.

When the punches just keep on coming the question has to be, what lesson am I still needing to learn? The punches will stop and the magic will begin again just as soon as the lessons have been learned.

# PART 4: LEARNING TO LOVE YOURSELF

### *Being Grateful*

If there is one thing in my life that I have trackable data for how it has impacted my life it is gratitude.

Like many I found *The Secret* by Rhonda Byrne in my long search of looking for just that. During my search for the secret on how to make my life better I found the book, then the film, then the power then the magic.

Like so many of the vast array of self-help methods that I tried, The Secret worked for a while. Apart from one thing, if I didn't attract what I wanted. I felt bad and it was so very focused on money that it felt icky to me and I began to repel money.

One thing I gained from this experience was gratitude.

I have books going back to 2012 where I have been grateful each day for 10 things, thanked the universe in advance for 10 things and then over time I added in forgiveness. When I first began doing this I was absorbed with it completely, and I can say that over those two years when this was part of my daily routine I grew my life in such a positive way. It helped me focus my days on the best that was happening. It helped me to keep grounded and in a positive mindset. When I look back at the times when things went not so well, they were the times I dropped this daily practice from my life; this added to the downward spiral.

For me being grateful is holding on to all that is good in our lives and thanking the universe for it. It is connecting with the energy of "thank you, thank you, thank you" for each thing. No matter where we are we all have things to be grateful for. Making the commitment to get up that little bit earlier each day to spend realistically 15-20 minutes doing this as a blessing and never a chore is key to me keeping my mindset focused on how lucky I am right now and how much growth there can be.

When things weren't going so well I had given up this positive habit and had allowed my mind to focus on lack. I was allowing myself to dwell on what had been lost, what was missing and it not only allowed my mind to go to some dark and awful places but also led to me losing even more.

My gratitude lists are something I like to handwrite, as there seems to be a greater connection to words and feelings by allowing my hand to have the words flow from them. I have an A5 book with quite thin lines to allow me two lines for each gratitude and some space at the bottom for the forgiveness.

This becomes my gratitude journal to track my progress. Each day that I do it the gratitude becomes easier and easier and I am able to forgive more and more of those around me and of myself.

The commitment to having a life that is lived from a place of gratitude is connected to what is called the Law of Attraction, which I do believe in, but I also believe it is so much more than the search for money and it cannot be relied upon alone. We must get up each day and take action towards the life that we want.

The energy that gratitude, true deep gratitude, created around us allows the universe to deliver more of what we want and deserve in life.

## Daring to Dream Again

Our thoughts shape and create our reality.

This is one of the simplest and yet most mind-blowing concepts.

Accepting that wherever I am in my life right now, every last bit of it, that I have created it, is a humbling part of this human experience that our souls are on. When things feel like they are going to shit faster than you can bring yourself to face them, this is a horrible realisation. In my darkest days I know that I blamed myself for how things were turning out in a very self-defeatist kind of way. The point I was missing was that, yes, I was and am responsible for the things that have gone wrong but I am also in charge of getting them to go well again.

When your life is going well it can seem to have an almost magical air about it. When you see people who seem to have all their shit together and things always seem to be going well for them, it can be easy to assume that they have always had it easy. The thing that I have come to realise is that other people's lives are none of my damn business.

If someone is doing well and living it up I am now able to feel super happy for them, rather than have that pang of jealousy, in fact in the most part I have always felt happy for others. Yes, while I was on my downward losing it all spiral of course I wondered why me... who the hell wouldn't have? If someone is going through hell, I wish them well, send them strength but know I have my own world to rebuild. I no longer feel the need to suspend my own healing and growth to step in and help.

The next stage, though, is so important.

It is essential that I learn to dream again. That I am able to get back to the days where I believed, where I knew that every dream can become a reality. Jeez I didn't just believe that stuff I created a plan to make it happen. I believed it with each beat of my heart.

The thing is when you feel like life has knocked the stuffing out of you. Where your greatest achievement in years feels like the fact that you have refused to throw yourself off a bridge, or write the letters and take a load of tablets with a bottle or three of wine... dreaming gets out of practice. Holding on becomes all that there is. There is a time and place for holding on. Without a darn doubt. In those moments of needing to hold on it is all you can expect of yourself and it is an achievement worth celebrating. When that passes, and I found once I decided to dig my heels in with life and come back up fighting I found the need to hold on began to pass remarkably quickly, once that phase has passed it could be easy to begin to plod.

Plodding is something I see lots of people doing in life. For some it is all they need to feel happy and I guess in a way that makes for a simple life. I am not now and never have been a plodder. I just don't have it in me. Maybe if I had have been a plodder I would have never left being an accountant and I'd have some fancy job now. Maybe if I'd have been a plodder I would have kept my house and not be in a tiny flat paying more than my mortgage used to be, but I created this reality for myself.

Sometimes I wonder if I created this reality for myself purely so that I would feel so uncomfortable in my own skin, in my own day-to-day existence that this book that I have been talking about since as long as I can remember would finally come pouring out of me. If it was then I sure hope this book goes on to help someone do something kinda awesome because it's been one awful, hellish and totally shitty path in getting to this point. One thing I do know is that I am all in committed to getting this out there and making this happen. I have once again yelled to the universe I am jumping, now come with me.

This isn't the first time that I have jumped. I have jumped a few times before and it has gone really well every time. I have the evidence in my life that I can dream and they come true. I have the experience of being supported in ways that seem almost too incredible to be believed. The only thing I would say is that once it started to go well, I scuppered myself.

When I dreamed before I dreamed what I thought I should dream, not my actual dreams, when I began to move things to get toward them I was easily side-tracked, I got injured and my internal narrative of "I'm not worthy" came up to bite me hard. I have learnt a lot in my journey to losing it all. I have learnt that I am worthy of happiness. I am worthy of love. I am worthy of whatever success I put my mind to and I am capable of it too. I have learnt that I am a bloody good mum. I might be a mum who lost her shit but I am a bloody good mum. I do not need anyone else to agree with that statement. I know it is true because of the awesome little ladies that my girls are growing into despite all we have been through.

I am ready to dream again.

The hardest part of me dreaming again is that my biggest dream is for a happy family. All I have ever really wanted is to have a home, be married, have happy children and to build memories with them. Everything else around that are the extras of life.

I used to feel the need to put all sorts of caveats on that or push it to one side because my marriage didn't work out. I used to think that because of this dream I had to put up with whatever my family did or said. For a long time I thought I had to make my life about a business dream because then I was in control.

Well, now I call bullshit. I call bullshit on myself. I don't have to make excuses for it. I don't have to water it down, I don't have to pretend or mask over my dream. My dream is to be in one of those relationships where you can see that the couple are meant to be together. When you feel it in your heart and soul. That is my dream. Whether that happens now or it's years away, I know with every beat of my heart that it is possible and it is what I deserve. I also know that I am the kind of woman that can light up someone's life. I deserve to be able to do that and to be with someone who wants to do that for me.

My unique brand of crazy is right for someone because I am ready. Not because I need it to be happy but because I am honest enough to know and admit that it's what I want and have always wanted.

So universe, I am ready to go all in on this one. I am ready.

The next dream I have always had is to help people. Nothing has ever made me feel as good and alive as when I have seen others transforming their lives and I have been able to support that. I first found this when I became a slimming coach. I adored doing this and I was very good at it. When I first set up my event, 'Realising Every Dream' I was in flow. My life was going where it needed to. I am not one who has a fear of speaking in public, not even in sharing the worst of me. I have always been able to be deeply honest and I know that it can help others.

Yes, this book is a big part of that. This book is me sharing the depths of my soul, the very worst of me, in the intention that it inspires others to take their own demons for a walk. None of us are perfect and in a world that seems so focused on the shallow, the fake and the seemingly perfect I am happy to stand in my totally imperfect, broken, messy, bat shit crazy but heart-sharingly open self.

It is my belief that if more of us could allow ourselves to fall apart. To sit with our own demons for a while we would each find peace. When we are able to truly accept that, in any moment we are capable of true love and also vile spite and we choose which way to turn. None of us are saints. None of us are gods. We are all unique individuals sent to earth to learn our lessons in the best way we can. Taking that time to allow ourselves to be the worst version of ourselves, to experience the darkest part of our soul and not shy away from it.

My dream is that I can help others heal from their pain and trauma by learning to own it.

My dream is also that one day I get to take my girls to Disney just like I sold my house to do. I want to see that magic in their eyes.

The thing I have realised about dreams and what makes them different to goals, isn't what so many of the little motivational memes say. A dream with a deadline does not become a goal.

A goal is something your own consistent action can take you to, with a reasonable degree of certainty. An example of this being; I want to be a size 12 by the summer. This is not in any way a dream. I have total control over how much I move my body and what and how much food I eat. The only impacting factors lie in my ability to achieve the goal. This is a goal that I am taking consistent action towards. I have chosen to set this as a body shape/size goal rather than a weight goal because I know that the number on that scale doesn't always reflect how I feel and I have been obsessed with this before. This time I want to make healthy life choices.

Having goals and the faith in myself to take action towards them and not give up at the slightest challenge is a very healthy thing. It is however NOT dreaming.

A dream is so much more than putting action steps in place.

For me a dream is something that is a little more out there. A little more requiring of the universe getting behind you. Something that needs a little bit of magic, luck, spark... divine intervention to it.

My question to you now is, what is your dream? Not your goal, not what you should want, is possible, realistic... what is your hand on heart dream?

## I Am in Love

I am in love.

I am in love with my life and the world around me.

This feeling is one that I have felt before. I have thrived on before and I have begun to harness before.

This feeling of being in love with life and the possibilities that lay before me is one that is most often seen in little children. It is the ability to revel in the littlest things, the ability to live in the moment that exists as it exists right now.

I am connected to all that I am and all that I have ever been. I feel a deep sense of gratitude for having been able to live through the things that I have and met the people that I have. I am no longer needing to question my past, cast doubt on myself or blame others. I just see everything as a journey that I have been graced with.

When I became a mum I found out for the first time in my life what love really was and is. That surge of energy that is so pure it almost feels like it is more than you are as a whole. I have always been willing to put all of me on hold for my girls. There is nothing I wouldn't do for them, nowhere I wouldn't go, nothing I wouldn't give, give up or go without. I have for the longest time lived and breathed for them.

For the first time I am now able to know that I feel the same for myself and for my life.

That is one very freeing feeling. It frees me from feeling that I am somehow a burden to my girls. I want them to grow up, seeing how they can love themselves and that it isn't selfish. That the first heart they must care for and trust is their own. That it isn't selfish it is fundamental.

As with many things it is not until you have it that you realise what was missing. Now that I do feel this deep profound love for myself I am amazed at some of the things I have allowed myself to put up with. Some of the foolish things I have done to myself. It is striking the difference between not feeling worthy and knowing that I am.

This feeling that I now have is the gift that I have received for the hard work of facing my personal depths and dark, sitting with my demons in the faith that they will not consume me. Sitting with them and learning to accept that they are just as much a part of me as the parts I adore and want the world to see.

This love that I am now able to feel I am struggling to understand how I ever made it through over 37 years without it.

Self-care and self-love seem to be such buzz terms at the moment and I have always taken it for granted that I must have loved myself. I have also taken self-care to be quite a practical thing; hair done, nails, a bubbly bath, good book, maybe some wine, a nice night out with friends, a walk along the beach, even investing a good therapist. That is all self-care, but none of it taught me self-love.

The reality is that I have made it through more than 37 years without self-love. I would even go as far as to say that at times I had self-loathing. I blamed myself for my mother's illness, for the way she and my father treated me, but all of these things were way out of my control. I was a child and I saved myself from that at 14 which is pretty incredible.

I have only ever been able to survive because that is all I was taught.

I was brought up in a house of drama, trauma, pain and judgement. Even when I did move away my grandparents' things were only physically better. They never taught me I was worthy, accepted or loved in the full meaning of love. That is not to say I am not eternally grateful to my grandparents for taking me in and allowing me to be away from my parents, just that they didn't teach me love either.

This journey I have been on which has taken me to places that have often felt like a living hell has brought me to somewhere I never realised I was missing. The most beautiful part is I know with certainty that I will ensure my daughters grow up with this. That they are able to love themselves, forgive themselves and own all of who they are.

This feeling is so strong and I have felt it before. I have felt it for others.

Why is it that we assume that we love ourselves and if it isn't always the case, why is this not taught?

Surely, when we love ourselves we look after ourselves more, we are more able to love and protect others then this can benefit everyone. Am I being too simplistic to wonder why our focus isn't on helping more people love themselves rather than simply gaining more material possessions?

I have had money. I have had a nice house, car, holidays, fancy shoes and none of it allowed me to feel like this.

All of the years of practicing gratitude helped me keep my mind in a positive place. Without a doubt, the times where I stopped this ritual directly correlated with the times where my outer world would take a nosedive. I have no doubt in the ability to create a better life by focusing on gratitude and taking action towards your goals.

The thing that I have lost in gaining this love of my self is fear. I am no longer scared to reach out to an old friend I've not spoken to in years. I am no longer scared to ask people I know to help. There is something mesmerising about this feeling. What I find the most fascinating and what I haven't had before is that I now have faith in myself. Even as a kid I always second guessed myself for fear of getting it wrong. I always had an internal battle to be able to get myself to do anything, until I can get myself so engrossed in something that it almost takes over and flows.

I have now lost that niggling voice of self-doubt. That almost constant inner voice that second guesses myself and makes it near impossible to make any choice with confidence. In fact the more I think back I do not ever think I have had confidence. I have feigned it well over the years but I have never had real confidence in myself. I have seen and heard the confidence of others in me and borrowed their belief for a while and I have had successes that I have been able to bounce from one to the other to keep momentum going. However, none of that is real self-confidence.

There is a subtle and quiet excitement about me now. I keep thinking that I haven't done too badly for myself at times in my life. I have never really had the backing of anyone else, least of all myself, and I have at points had a rather lovely life. I am excited to see what I can do and what I can achieve with this newfound love.

Love is something that is without doubt abundant. It doesn't lessen as you give it, show it, share it. I am excited to see just how much

I can love myself, those around me and what I will be able to make happen from this space.

Who knew that the most important person I had to fall in love with was never anyone else but myself?

Or maybe it's one of those things that we are told but we never believe until you experience it.

## *I Am so Sorry*

There is a wonderful and awful realisation that hits when you realise you have never loved yourself. The feeling when you first begin to love yourself and that energy arrives is simply amazing, it is better than the best rollercoaster, night of dancing, comedy show, or wild sex ever. It has a kind of light giddy height that I am blessed to be feeling.

I no longer feel like I am searching. I feel complete and I feel whole.

Along with the feeling of completeness is the realisation that I wasn't complete before.

I had spent much of my life unknowingly looking to have this space, this part of me that only I could fill, to be created by loving someone else. In that process I have hurt myself many times because I have often fallen in love with others who also do not love themselves. This I am less sorry for as those people, they are just as much part of that as I was. We no doubt hurt each other and we can both learn from that.

I am so sorry to the couple of people who weren't searching. They already did love themselves and tried to love me. It has only happened once, possibly twice in my life. I have generally attracted those who, like me, were broken... or 'missing' as I prefer to call it. Missing self-love.

There are bound to be others too that I have hurt. If not through my actions towards them but in seeing me allow myself to get hurt time and time again and always go back for more.

Each time I felt like I had a broken heart I have always tried to do the work to fix myself before looking for love again. Well, I say always but maybe not every time, I have rebounded a few times too. It was never my intention to hurt anyone, not myself and not those that I care about and love.

My intention for my whole life has always been to be a good person. In fact that need to be a good person has probably held me back as much, if not more, than the fact that until recently I had no idea what it felt like to love myself.

If I have ever hurt you I am so sorry.

If you have every hurt me, I say thank you. From the absolute bottom of my heart I am so very grateful for the lesson.

I am in no doubt that without each of the attempts at love, without each of the friends, partners even business partners over the years I would have never reached the point where I know what it feels like to actually love myself.

I am so sorry for the pain I have caused and I hope and wish that you are able to learn the lesson in our paths crossing that I have been able to do.

In my time I have met and loved some incredible people. I have also met some shocking people who have torn not just my world but the worlds of others apart. I have loved people who always told me they could never be there and only ever remained true to that. I have loved people who never even cared for me and only put on an act to get what they wanted. I have loved people who have seemed to take joy in my pain. I have also failed to love people who have loved me truly and deeply and I am so very very sorry for that.

I could not give anyone more than I could give myself.

I now know what I was missing and what I was unable to give others. I hope that you have found that somewhere else and can find it in your heart to forgive me.

My core belief is that we are all here to heal and learn. My path to healing has been challenging to say the least. I know that I have never at any point intended to hurt anyone else, I simply do not have that in me, it doesn't meet with the fundamental part of who I am and always have been. Lack of intent does not mean that there haven't been people that have been hurt in my journey to healing and learning to deeply love myself.

A large part of learning to love myself has been learning to show myself compassion, kindness and forgiveness. It is not as easy as it sounds when you are used to being your own biggest critic. I hope that in time you can forgive me if I have ever hurt you and accept my thanks for your part in my journey to finding my heart and making it whole.

## Fear-Based Decision-Making

My whole life, well the 37 years of it up until now, I have made most of my decisions from a place of fear. I never knew this until I was able to stand back from my life long enough to really dig deep into who I am, why I do the things I do and take stock.

The time to do this is something I never thought I would have. I was always busy. When you are busy you're so into the doing of things that the time to stand back and question it all would be near impossible to find. Maybe that is why I was always so busy.

Having the time and the type of mind that questions everything, that is always looking for the deeper meaning of everything has led me to a conclusion that all of my major decisions have been done from a place of fear.

Fear is a basic emotion that we all feel. My childhood was perpetuated with fear. I was always scared. I couldn't recognise it at the time and it is only with deep reflection that I am able to see that I lived in a permanent state of fight or flight. It's not surprising with a manic and potentially psychopathic mother.

What I have only begun to realise is that this constant fight or flight had remained with me. I had then gone on to choose situations that felt comfortable. For me comfortable was being in fight or flight. I have always been the calm one in a crisis. It is one of my skills and I can always see solutions, I don't freak out at all and can deal with it. Well, of course, I had to tread on eggshells 24/7 to be sure I didn't set my mum off and if she did blow I had to be calm so as not to make it worse.

These are all things that can be read about from any adult who has grown up in a toxic/abusive/neglectful home. The thing that I have never read about, and I have read around the topic a lot, is that the fear-based decision-making has continued.

When I say this what I mean is that each time I make a major life decision I make it from a place of fear, fight or flight. I am able to make huge decisions quickly but they are not coming from a place of love, they are coming from a place of fear.

- I didn't go to Essex University to study Politics because I was scared my boyfriend and I would split up.
- I married my ex-husband 18 days after I found out he had pawned a family heirloom ring. I married him because I was scared of being a single mum, I was 36 weeks pregnant.
- I didn't promote my matchmaking business as much as I had the skills and knowledge to because I was scared of failure and being judged.

These are just three examples of huge life choices which, if I had had the confidence to believe in myself, in love, in life and not live from a place of fear, I could have decided differently. I might have even still made the same choices, but my hand on heart reason would have been healthier.

Even when I look at the smaller decisions in life I have often been motivated more by fear. Fear and panic seem to be my biggest motivators. The Ted talk *Inside the mind of a procrastinator* by Tim Urban that is so funny. I urge you to watch it as I have never seen anything that is so like me and even if it's not like you it is worth the 15 minutes for the laughs alone.

The funniest thing about the whole thing is that he says that he talks about how study is planned and then all done at the end. He talks about the thesis and how he ended it up doing it in 72 hours, he joked that they called and said it was the best one they ever saw. He goes on to say that his was not good. What struck me here was I really did do mine in four days, pulling all-nighters and I got 86%, which is incredible at degree level. I was told it was a PHD level bit of work. BUT this only comes out when I am in total panic.

This is not to say that I do not make healthy choices, I do.

I have made lots of healthy choices in my life. However if I look at them, even the healthy choices have been made from a place of fear.

What happens when decisions are made from a place of fear? This is not the same as the fear of making decisions.

One of the things I know is that I have said "yes" to lots of things that with hindsight or even basic consideration for my own needs, dreams and hopes, I shouldn't have agreed to. The fear of being judged, the fear of not being considered a good person, friend, mother, worker often leads me to saying "yes" when if I just had the confidence in myself, the love for myself and my life I would much more likely have said "yes" anyway but felt better in doing so.

In essence, fear-based decisions have been a way that I have put my needs, wants and desires to the bottom of the list. It doesn't cross my mind to say "no". It doesn't cross my mind to consider the impact of adding in yet another task, "where there is a will there is always a way" was my motto for the longest time.

The fear of judgement has always had a huge impact on me. The fear that if I say "no" to someone I care about they will not care anymore. The fear that I will do something that I really want to do and be shamed for it. That I will get pulled apart for it. Here is the thing though, even when I tried to protect myself from all of that judgement and losing people, I was still judged. I still lost almost everybody.

Building a life based on fear is like building a house on sand rather than solid foundations; sooner or later it is all going to fall down. Now I have realised that I have been operating from a fear-based assessment of life it makes it so much easier to change. After all, we cannot change what we cannot see.

What was the magical piece in me that allowed me to see this? The kind of key to my suffering, if you will? It has been the realisation that I had never loved and accepted myself. That I learned by doing the work to get to truly love and accept myself.

I can pinpoint the exact moment that love for myself landed within me. Much like I have seen the moment that I have fallen in love with others, it has always been unexpected and something seemingly insignificant which almost tips the balance into love.

Once I have been able to feel that deep love and acceptance of myself I have been able to look back at my life with the advantage of time and with a perspective previously unavailable to me.

I can only imagine that the opposite must also be possible. For those who are brought up with a solid sense of self, who are shown how to love themselves and cater for their needs, if ever they find themselves not loving themselves it too could feel like finding a whole new room in a house you thought you knew every part of.

Learning to take a step back from decisions and take the time to consider carefully what I truly want and how it makes me feel is a new dimension to my life that I am thriving on. What I am finding most striking is that the time and effort that would have been put into helping those that I care about with their decisions I am now putting into myself.

There is no feeling of panic, of what if I get it wrong when it comes to making decisions. Nor am I backing away from them and half leaving them up to fate. I am relishing the opportunity to take the helm of my life and become the active decision-maker in it. It is breathing a new passion back into me that allows me to see there is a world of opportunity out there.

One of the decisions I used to leave to other people that I no longer will, is who I chose to have in my life. For the longest time I thought so little of myself that I felt this sense of wow, they like me? A kind of shock that anyone would want me in their lives. I thought so little of myself and had such a low value on my time and presence that I have always made myself almost the second-class citizen within any relationship.

That isn't healthy, not for anyone. That is not a healthy basis for a friendship, family or partnership. That ability to allow myself to be walked all over can bring out the worst in people. I have allowed it to happen, no, I have actively participated in training people to treat me the way I thought I was worthy of.

That won't be the case anymore.

Now that I am able to love myself and make decisions from that place I can see the value in my time, my presence and that I have a lot to offer other people and situations.

Now the fun begins in deciding who and when I want to create, recreate or accept new challenges.

The biggest difference I can see between fear-based decision-making and love-based decision- making is that when you are able to make decisions from a place of love and peace rather than fear and panic, there is a joy in the possibility. There is a joy in what could be, what might be, a wonder, if you will. Whereas when things are born from a place of fear there is always a trepidation that something is about to go wrong. When you keep looking for what might go wrong... you will always find it.

I am done with looking for what might go wrong. I have lived through all of my greatest fears. I have faced the hell of my nightmares and I have come out the other side victorious. The victory being that I have finally learnt to not only love myself, but also to begin to face the challenge of this life and what remains of it, with the joy of choosing every part of my life from a place of love and an expectation of what can go right. Underpinned with the total faith that no matter what could go wrong, I know I can handle it because I have survived much worse already.

If 37 years of being fearful have created some pretty awesome times with a whole host of awful then my reckoning is that the next 37 will be the balancing act of a world of wonderfulness with some dashes of wonky just to keep me grounded.

I am excited for the future, for the life that I am about to create. One love-based decision at a time.

## Looking Deeper

I have always looked deeper at everything. I can't help it, I'm not one of those people who can just laugh it off, let it go and live on the surface of life. I have to question things, read up on them, learn around the experience and challenge it.

When I was at school I wanted to be a Barrister because they basically argue a point for a living and I have always known there are many ways to look at any situation. To me a debate is not only healthy, it is fun. One of my favourite things is being able to talk for hours about why things are a certain way, to look into the deeper meaning of things. I enjoy being challenged and thinking things through a different way, I am open to learning a new viewpoint and that it could blow mine out of the water. For me this is a way of learning. I am not precious about my thoughts and opinions at all, they are there to be explored. Not many people like to do this I have found. Many are so protective over their opinions that they will defend them as they are an extension of themselves. I generally don't get on well with these people.

In my life I have only ever met a handful of people who love to talk about the deep things in life as much as I do. Maybe it's one of the reasons I've begun to talk to less people. I get so bored with the superficial pleasantries I can't be bothered to put my energy to it. I can feel a superficial, fake or just for show conversation from a mile away and it repels me. I'd prefer to be genuinely nice to someone and brighten their day than pretend to be nice to someone.

Being deep allows me to look at the challenges that life can throw in a very different perspective. I look at things on two levels, the here and now, day-to-day practical way of surviving, healing or growing from it, and then from the ask - what is the wider life lesson here and how is this going to help my life improve long-term?

Splitting this into two levels like this allows me to find positivity even in the darkest times. I have always said to my girls that I believe without doubt that we have all learnt so much in the last few years. Lessons none of us wanted but ones that we couldn't have learnt another way. I truly believe that one if not all of us will one day do something with those lessons that will be incredible. That we will one day look back and say, "wow, I couldn't have done this if I hadn't have lived through that."

That level of hope when living through the tough and rough stuff in life is like a life raft. It is delayed gratification to the max!

Looking deeper into how and why things happen or are happening has allowed me to take responsibility for the things that I have done to create it. Always looking to see where I have made choices that I wouldn't make again ensures I am learning the lessons and not going to go into a repeat cycle of the universe saying, "are you not listening to me?"

We are not all born the same. We are all born with a different set of circumstances. If you are born into a loving, kind, supportive family you do without doubt get a head start in life.

However if you aren't, if you are born into any level of destructive, dysfunctional, abusive family then you get a whole heap of lessons that those with the head start don't. One of the biggest is - do you use that as an excuse to mess up your life? Or do you choose to learn from it and grow?

My belief here is that if you live through a family which doesn't give you the boundaries, stability and life foundations that we all deserve then there is a high chance that at some point you're going to realise that you are making some rubbish choices. That is OK.

When I look back at some of the relationship choices I have made in my life, from my marriage to even some of my friendships, I had co-created my childhood. I had created what I was used to.

That is natural and normal.

This is why those who are brought up with healthy, stable, loving relationships around them find it so much easier and are more successful early on in their lives in creating the same. They had the example. This was no huge success for them. Most likely if they begin to date someone who comes from a dysfunctional family, they will walk away because it doesn't fit with their life experience.

Whereas two people who have both had dysfunctional childhoods are going to attract each other and what would be red flags to others, they let slide. I was always such a saver. I wanted to save everyone and totally missed the point in my life that the person I needed to save all along was myself.

This is very common in relationships. I believe it's one of the biggest reasons for so many failing relationships. Adults who haven't dealt with a traumatic, dysfunctional childhood are highly unlikely to be able to build healthy, happy and stable relationships around them. How could they? They have never been taught. This isn't taught in school. They weren't taught at home.

Yet society just expects us to go out and create the most important unit without any help or support. The family is without doubt the most important unit in the human life. Everyone seems to blame their parents for something, some with total justification. I, however, thank mine. I thank both my parents for showing me all that I do not want to be. I am eternally grateful that I can look back at the things they both did, now with adult perspective, without the opinions of others around me clouding my perspective, and shine that back into what my girls are now living through. It would be so easy to blame them and without doubt both were selfish, unstable and abusive parents. However, they are not to blame for what I chose to do with my life after that.

I chose to remain in contact with my mother, even though she was always sucking the life out of me. I made that choice to keep her in my life and allow her to trigger me. No one else. That is my responsibility. I could have walked away sooner. When I did walk away, I could have been stronger and stayed away. Not felt the need to drop my life to save her each time.

That is one lesson that the universe served me over and over, with harsher and harsher consequences. Learn to walk away from those who harm you. Especially those who show no remorse, guilt or willingness to change.

I never learnt how to have my needs met. I was actually shown that my needs didn't matter. As long as the ticking time bomb that was my mentally unstable mum didn't explode that was all that mattered. That was true when I was a child and again at 36. The fallout onto me and my life was never considered, not as a child and not as a woman with children who were and are also impacted.

The responsibility here was not for my mum to change. It was for me to walk away and stay away. I had escaped at 14 and at 21 but always gave in to the opinions of others and went back. My biggest lesson here: to learn to trust myself. I know my world, my life better than others. While a debate is great, no one knows my life, my world better than me and no opinion no matter how well expressed surpasses that.

I am the expert of my own life.

I know the depths of my life and the lessons it has blessed me with. Looking deeper into our own lives opens up many opportunities to learn and grow.

# PART 5: SPIRITUALITY

## *11:11*

It all began with 11:11.

I began to see 11:11 everywhere, not just the time but everywhere. I looked it up and thought that the 11.11 wish was a lovely idea to do with my little ladies, they were tiny and we loved all things magical so this fitted well.

My spiritual journey was beginning with angel numbers. Next I learnt that I am an empath. Then I read *The Secret* and began to practice gratitude.

My life became rather wonderful. Everything I dreamed of began to become true. I worked hard too, I didn't just expect it to land because I wished. I was all aboard the Law of Attraction train. Full steam ahead.

Little did I know that this was the most whimsical entry to my spiritual journey that I could have wished for. I am super grateful for it because these years showed me that what we focus on we create. I saw it, felt it, experienced it and lived it for myself. I didn't need to put blind faith into a book, a movie or a speaker I had lived it.

It was a wonderful, magical time and some of the happiest times of my life have happened during 2012 to 2014. I tried with *The Secret*, found it too money focused, loved *The Magic* and *The Power* was without doubt my favourite. I thought I was on a spiritual journey.

I read Wayne Dyer, Louise Hay, I threw myself into learning about Buddhism. There can be no doubt I was searching. I was ready to dig a little dipper on this ride we call life. I wanted to connect more, to feel more to be more. I also got into personal development and began going to seminars where everyone seemed to have the magic answer, the system, the process that would change everything. I was so ready to believe that. For a while I was all in on it.

When my life fell to pieces I needed something to grab on to, a life raft I guess and I looked more and more into spirituality. I did courses each month, I saw a homeopath, I tried to be vegan. I learnt to meditate. I learnt tarot cards, energy protection, healing about crystals - all things that were fascinating to learn about.

What I couldn't see was that the more and more I searched outside of myself the more and more confused I became with it all. The more it became conflicting and I agreed with some parts and not with others, I scratched the surface with some things but never delved deep enough to get anywhere meaningful.

My spiritual journey and if you read well you will see the same thing time and time again, all of the most authentic teachers are saying the same. The journey to your soul is not one that you can be guided to. The journey to your soul is not found in a book, a lecture hall, on Ted talks, or anywhere outside of you.

The journey to finding the core of who we are is an internal journey.

The hardest and the most rewarding thing I have been able to do is to get ok with being alone. I mean really alone, no TV, no reading, no mobile phone scanning through, no chats with this friend, that friend, the neighbours.

No turning on Netflix and letting it go from one episode to the next, then the next, then the next... actually that one did happen a few times! I am only human. Getting quiet with myself. Asking myself the questions I did know the answers to and allowing myself to be heard, explored and trusted, that is the most spiritual thing I have ever done.

In a world so full on constant noise, business, demands, pace, push and motion, the time to sit and allow myself to just be was incredible. At times it was dark. At times it was scary. At times I didn't like what I found inside my mind, inside my soul There were thoughts that scared the hell out of me. There was a level of anger at the world, justified anger, I really do feel that needed to come out.

I had to stop masking. I had to stop striving, I had to stop pretending to be all that I thought I should be. I had to stop looking outside of myself for the answers.

I put myself on a reading ban. I love books. I only allowed myself to watch comedy videos not motivational, personal development videos for a while. I needed to get to know myself. What I thought, felt, believed, and give myself the time to get to know me. This was a journey that I had begun in 2014 and I was ready to take the next stage.

Back in 2014 I had spent 8 months dating myself. I stopped putting all of my effort into dating and put that same effort into me. I took myself to the same places you do when you date, I went to the movies, to see comedy, for meals and I ended up taking myself to Rome. It was incredible. I learned to love myself, or so I thought. I would say now I learned to value myself because much like lots of the dating I did that was quite superficial. I had not allowed myself the vulnerability to go inwards.

Now was my time to go for it again but this time I didn't get myself all dressed up, I didn't take myself out. Partly because I had managed to lose every penny I had ever earned up to that point but I am now seeing even that as a blessing. My true spiritual journey began when I removed all distractions. When I created a life that was so basic I could either wallow in it or dig deeper on myself. I took myself out of the networks, groups and academies I had been part of. I withdrew from friends and most interactions. I began to search my own soul.

This was not the most fun experience of my life. I cannot deny that going to the cinema, comedy and Rome was a darn sight more fun than this inward journey. It wasn't pretty and it wasn't fun. It took every ounce of faith that I had to keep looking at myself to see why I had done the things that I had.

At each stage in this process I kept getting little signs that I was on the right path. White feathers seemed to float in front of me, a robin kept crossing my path. I got a message from my grandad who'd passed a few years before saying he was proud of how I was living my life and the love that I was showing others.

I had to pull back from the charity that I was on the board for. I had to stop being so darn busy and get to know myself. I had to accept that each time I tried to help others before I had healed myself it was little more than a distraction.

I cried. Oh my word did I cry. I cried over photos, I cried over times I wish I could get back. I laughed, I laughed at some of the wonderful silly things I had done in the moments where I allowed me to trust myself. Where I had found that fleeting inner faith to jump and live and be caught by the universe.

I began to write. I began to write this book and trusted that every word I would commit to the page was pure and from my own unique heart and had a message that was worthy of being heard. I learned to believe in me. I spent time meditating on some of the best times in my life and some of the worst times. I am not good at silent meditation. I found guided meditations that allowed me to explore myself and let go of the constraints I had put on myself or allowed others to put on me.

I began to live again.

It all began with 11:11 when I first began to realise that there is more to this world than the physical. There is more to our world than what we can see and touch. Our 3D reality is only one tiny part of what this universe has to offer us. Our soul is only in this body for this human experience, we have been here before and if we are brave enough we do get to do it again and choose some different lessons.

My lesson, my overarching lesson on this merry-go-round of the human experience? It is so simple and so complex all at once. It is something I have heard a million times but only learnt through searching my soul to find what I was missing.

Learning to love yourself, every last part of you is all there really is.

There is nothing more to this life than that. Learning to love and accept every last part of who I am. What I have done, been and am capable of. It sounds so simple.

Love yourself.

Those two words have more depth in them than the deepest ocean, more beauty than the most breathtaking sunset and more pain than your worst memory.

It is so easy to think that we love ourselves. It is a whole other thing to be able to look inside and take total responsibility for each and every moment in your life. The day, no, the moment I accepted that I chose this life, that I am responsible for it all, I stopped being a victim and I became a spiritual badass.

It all began with 11:11.

## Being an Empath

I am an Empath.

The first time I read about what an empath was it sounded all kind of spooky. It was on an empath support group that I found online in 2012. I had always known what empathy was. To be empathetic towards someone else is a widely accepted thing. However, when I read this list and then I took the test, I was so relieved when the answer came out that I am an empath. It seemed to answer so much for me.

I feel everything. I was once told that I feel the planets move, which to a point I do.

If we are at a party, I can feel when there is going to be an argument before it happens. In a club I could always sense it before it happened and generally get my friends away. I know if someone is lying to me, I know in my gut if they are covering something up. Sadly until recent years I have also tended to project goodness on to people and assume the very best in them.

I get absolutely exhausted by people. Being in large groups drains me because it is like system overload, I am noticing everything and feeling it all too. For the longest time I absorbed the feelings of others so strongly that often I couldn't distinguish between their feelings and mine. I would spend time around someone and it would all feel a certain way. When I saw a lot of them I would think I felt a certain way but after a while my own feelings became clear and it would be so different it would leave me confused.

It has been a challenging journey to find out more about what this means for me. Partly as I do have quite a logical mind and the thought that I can feel others, sometimes clearer than they are able to articulate for themselves, has been scary.

Learning how to manage this so that I don't lose all of my energy has been a big part of my process in learning to be all of myself. During my journey I have ended up being around people who to me seemed like "more of" an empath than me and my mind would slip into inferiority. Much like with my spiritual journey I would often feel "not as" spiritual as someone. This is all rubbish, there is no comparison or competition with this stuff. We are all just as we need to be and perfect in this moment.

The key skills I have learnt to make walking this earth as an empath easier are:

1. Accept that not everyone gets what an empath is.
2. Learn to ground your energy regularly. This can be done in a number of ways from imagining your energy going into the earth like the roots of a tree, or an anchor going to the core of the earth. Stepping out into nature, putting your feet into the sea, walking barefoot outside or simply asking to be grounded now.
3. Cut cords regularly to ensure you are not attached to energetic links that do not serve you.
4. Connect with others who have the same sensitive souls and understand.
5. Learn more about the universe, energies and planets, and trust what feels right is so.
6. Meditate and make it an essential daily practice - I get on best with guided meditations.
7. Clear the energy in your home with either sage, incense or essential oils in a diffuser.

8.   Make time to be alone, rest and recharge after time with people.

9.   Exercise to get excess energy out of my body.

Being an empath means that I find it near impossible to watch the news and see others in pain, I feel that pain. Horror films are a no-go zone because I am beyond jumpy and scared.

I often find that near strangers will tell me their deepest secrets.

I am terrible at shallow conversations. I just can't talk about the weather, day-to-day chitter chatter bores me beyond belief and I will often end up talking about something much deeper than most people would.

I care so much about other people I have had to learn the hard way that it's not selfish to cater for my needs first. I have had to learn that it is my responsibility and mine alone to look after my energy so that I have enough for it to be overflowing.

I have a deep desire to help the world move to a place where every human gets a decent life. Where we are all equal and not beholden purely to money. I feel a deep sense of injustice in our world and want to be a part of creating something where we all get to be happy and feel loved.

Being an empath is a blessing but it can be exhausting.

I am so grateful to all of the beautiful souls I have connected with around the globe who are also empaths or sensitive, old souls. The healing that we are able to create when we connect is hugely powerful and is creating a stronger light for others to be able to see and link in with.

One of the beauties of the world we live in is we are able to connect with each other more than in any time in our history. Distance does not mean much. Empaths around the world are able to share experiences, support each other and raise the collective vibration each day.

It is a gift to be able to feel so much and learning to manage that in a way which allows us to be your best and keep serving the world around us without diminishing ourselves is a skill.

One of my favourite ways to pick my vibe back up after I encounter someone who drains me greatly is to pop on some music that makes me feel good again. Ideally I would drink more water and be vegan but for now I am still a coffee-drinking carnivore.

For now I am still very much a work in progress and making my way towards being able to harness this energy more.

## *Writing my Future*

Each day I get up I am writing my future.

Each time I choose what to drink, eat, how much to move my body, I am writing the story of my future health.

Each day I get up and choose to smile on the way to work, write gratitude lists and focus on the wonderful things in my life I am creating my state for that day. My state each day affects how I react to the things around me.

Each time I decide to let more and more of my past go I create room for the future I want to arrive.

Each time I choose to meditate rather than scroll and scroll on social media adds to the calm in my mind and expands rather than contracts my consciousness.

Each time I work to connect with my higher self and spirit I open myself up the possibility that I can create my future.

Each time I choose to accept my past I am no longer its prisoner.

Each time I connect with someone in the faith that I am bringing my light to them I give life to any number of possibilities.

Each time I choose to be grateful for everything I have been up until now I take away the power of the past.

Each time I refuse to blame anyone or anything for my life I take total responsibility for my future.

Each time I get up and I take action towards the future that I dream of I put more distance between the prison of my thoughts and get closer to the magic of the universe.

Each time I choose to live the moment that is now and trust that what is coming out of me is meant to I put my faith in to the universe.

Each time I choose to be thankful to every person who has ever crossed my path I welcome new people and experiences.

Each time I look at all I have and refuse to connect with the energy of what I had I make space for new to arrive.

Each time I look in the mirror and choose to focus on my beauty and not my flaws my attractiveness grows.

Each time I choose to be grateful for my body, health and energy I send love into my body which helps it heal and flourish.

Each time I am deeply grateful for being a mum I quietly share love with my girls that they feel no matter where they are.

Each time I silence the doubts that me writing each day isn't the path for me and I get up and I write anyway I take a step closer to that which my heart knows is my destiny.

Each time I feel the rush of love in my heart where it feels like my heart is expanding just a little when I think of someone but I don't push it down thinking it's too much, too soon, I allow that feeling to remain natural.

Each time I remind myself that I am worth so much more than my bank account I allow for more finances to arrive as I know I am worthy.

Each time I realise that I am deeply happy right now in this very moment I allow for more happiness to arrive.

Each time I see my children are incredibly happy even though I have the least to give them materially than I have ever had I realise I am raising incredible human beings.

Each time we stop because we see a feather somewhere unusual I am grateful for learning more about messages from angels.

Each time I see a robin redbreast I know that it's my grandad stopping by to remind me how proud he is of me and that he knows I will be a success and that he wants me to keep going.

Each time I trust myself to allow the words to type out onto the page without the filter of my mind I am reminded that this book is my purpose.

Each time I write about my past I know that it is not to say "poor me" in any way, it is because this is my gift. My gift is to show that anyone can go through hell and come out an even kinder person.

Each time I am honest about how far I pushed myself in fear of being judged I allow others to say that they need help.

Each time I admit that I'm the mum who didn't get help and hurt her daughter, I show the importance of asking for help and allowing yourself to be vulnerable.

Each time my girls and I are connected with a deep love and respect I show that anyone can screw up and still make it right.

Each time I own my flaws I become stronger.

Each time I refuse to go back to those who tried to shame, belittle or judge me I own my own power and light.

Each time I keep going even though my past choices keep showing up just reminds me how far I have come.

Each time I laugh until my belly hurts with my girls and they look at me with a kind of gaze I've never seen before I know that for the things I did wrong. I also did a million things right.

Each time I trust in the process of the universe a miracle appears.

Each time I allow myself to be all of me I become more and more of the best of me.

Each time I let go of the fear of how I am going to pay the bills I create the space for me to create something more.

Each time I appreciate the good times I welcome more of them.

Each time I look for the lesson in the shitty times I let it go more.

Each time I think of a person from my past with love, compassion and kindness I let them go more and become more free.

Each time I allow myself to be helped and supported by those around me I deepen my connection with them.

Each time I focus my energy on creating a beautiful future I become closer to it.

Each time I accept that everyone is flawed I open my heart to the world around me.

Each time I commit to not judging others, even those who have judged me I lessen anyone's power over me.

Each time I am willing to look at every experience as a reflection of myself I am able to see just how awesome and awful I can be.

Each time I accept my awful and celebrate my awesome I become happier.

Each time I stop looking outside of myself for the answers I become more whole.

Each time I have the guts to ask for help I allow others into my life.

Each time I look after myself I show the universe I am worthy of good things, people and experiences flowing back into my life.

Each time I let go of the past I allow my future to be created.

Each time I trust myself to write this book I take myself closer and closer and closer to my future.

Each time I trust that I will be able to make it through the practical of getting published and before the people who need to read this the closer I come to that reality.

Each time I say I don't care if I am judged for the contents of this book the faster it flows.

Each time I think of the moment I knew I had to write it the fuller of love I feel and I know it's the right thing.

Each time I think of all the signs in my life that I was going to do this I smile because it's been a long time coming and I fought this process for so long and made it vastly more hard work and arduous than it needed to be.

Each time I doubt myself I look at all the shit I have lived through, all the times I never thought I could survive, all the times it felt like my heart was being shattered into a million pieces and how I have always put myself back together again.

I am here for a reason and for now my reason is this book.

I didn't sink, I learnt to swim!

If it weren't for all of the awful things I wouldn't be who I am right now. Who I am right now is someone who knows how to heal from the worst pain and wants to give that hope and faith to anyone swimming their own moat right now. I made it through and I am nothing special. If I can make it through I promise you, you can too.

I have finally learnt to love myself and in that am able to love you too. Learning to sit with the shitty parts of myself, my past, my personality has at times been a lonely journey but it is the most important one any of us can do.

Who cares about journey to centre of the earth, this is journey to the centre of your soul.

Anyone who can love and accept even the darkest parts of their soul can love and accept anyone and anything.

I would walk this path a million times if it got me back to here. I am writing my future.

## I am the Expert of my Life

I love the field of personal development. I have read lots, been to seminars, hosted seminars, and worked with mentors and coaches.

It took me the longest time to realise that while having a coach or a mentor is something I passionately believe in, they are not the expert of my life. I am blessed to have had some fabulous coaches and mentors in my life and the phrase "you are the expert of your own life" comes from the wonderful Kate Spencer who was my energy coach in 2015. If you are in any way looking to delve deeper into your spiritual side but want someone whose feet are firmly on the ground she is your lady.

I had to reach the lowest of the low, rock bottom and then some before it hit me. I already know what I need to do. I have always know what I need to do but I stopped listening. I began looking outside of myself for the answers.

There is a fine line between:

looking for guidance - healthy

And looking to be told what to do - unhealthy.

When I look back to the points in my life where I have done exactly what felt right at that time, trusting my own heart and soul without the need for validation from others. I have always won.

When at 14 I got myself moved to my grandparents - saved my own life.

When at 21 I got myself homed away from my mother - again saved my life.

When at 28 I knew my marriage was ending and I was going to be a single mum with 2 babies under 3, I passed my driving test, set up a business, ran a ½ marathon and lost weight all within 6 months.

When at 29, I gave up my full-time job as an accountant to focus on my business because that allowed me to be with my babies every day and never miss a single part of their young childhood.

When at 32 I took on a degree even though I'm dyslexic, going on to prove statistically that dyslexia is a benefit in business.

When at 34 I set up an event called 'Realising Every Dream' with speakers and performers to help show people they can achieve anything they dare to dream of.

All of these things I did and I did well through believing in my own heart. No one had to tell me to do them and they all worked out brilliantly for me.

Alongside these there are the choices I made that didn't work out well.

When at 25 I chose to marry a man I knew had gambled all we had, pawned my jewellery and lied to me about it with no shame, guilt or remorse.

When at 27 I flew out the same day to care for my mentally ill mother in Spain even though my baby was 10 weeks old.

When at 34 I chose not to ask friends for help with my girls after an injury because I was too proud.

When at 35 I sold my house to be able to take my girls to Disneyland and invest in my business.

When at 36 I trusted my mum to buy a house with me even after she'd made us homeless once before.

The thing is with all of these choices, the good, the awful and everything in between, I made them with full knowledge of my life. The good ones took my life to places that were wonderful. They brought about the happiest times of my life, where I felt in flow. Where the laughs were abundant and the memories are still magical.

The choices I made from my own heart that didn't work out so well, because I made them from my heart have all taught me something.

If I were to go back now, I would still marry my ex-husband. My daughters are the best part of my life, they are my favourite people in this world and without him I wouldn't have them and I would not change that for anything. Also marrying him taught me so very much. I am deeply grateful for that experience in its totality.

Flying to and from Spain for 2 months while my daughters were 22 months and 3 months old was horrific. My mum was so severely mentally ill she was accusing me of trying to kill her and I was genuinely scared I'd be arrested. She never slept, which meant I never slept and in the end we had to get her sedated, flown home and put into a UK mental health unit. At hospital she managed to appear "normal" until I stepped into the room and she was so vile and aggressive they agreed to admit her. If I were to go back now, this I wouldn't do. This I would let her sister, who now claims to be there for her, or her parents do. This I wish I'd stepped back from because it was always a one-way street. However this has now taught me that some people will take everything from you and still make you out to be the bad guy.

Not asking for help. This is one thing I would change if I could. I was always so quick to help others. So quick to say "yes", to drop everything for those I love and care about. I now know that I had never been taught I would get help. Throughout my life I was there to save my mum, grandparents, anyone I cared for, and no one ever saved me. Learning to trust others to be there for me is a lesson I am still learning today. This is without doubt my work in progress.

Selling my house. This is one thing that now we have nothing I have to let go of. At the time it was the right decision. Something good will come from this lesson, keeping the faith here, that is a lesson in itself.

Trusting my mum again, her letting us down again. This was my final lesson in how she would do anything to destroy me. There is no love there, there never has been, never will be and she would not give a second thought if I was alive or dead. To hear her mental health support team say that my ability to even try to trust her again was testimony to the work I had done has always remained with me. I know I worked hard and tried with my mum all my life, but it was such a one-way street that can't be allowed to continue. I have to put my life before hers, for mine and my girls' sake.

Looking outside of myself and not trusting myself does not help me to grow. In each moment I do know what is the best thing to do. I always have because in the things that turned out well there are a number of times where my choices have literally saved my life. Then in some of the others I have been told that I have saved a life... now that is an incredible feeling to be told that someone is off suicide watch because of something you created. I'd put that up there as one of the best feelings in all this world.

There have also been times where I have listened so much to those around me that I have second guessed myself. Not listened to my own heart and soul and ended up in some mighty rubbish places. No matter how well trained, experienced or qualified anyone is they cannot know my life.

To keep looking outside wasn't what I needed. I had a few coaches that were brilliant. Coaching wasn't what I needed at that time. I needed to let go from my past, forgive myself and others, and be ready to set sail again without the weight of the past but with the gems of the lessons.

I am ready to keep being the expert of my life and I truly hope that some of my lessons can help others begin to take ownership and step into being the experts of their lives.

In learning to trust myself I am also learning to tap into my intuition and the direct link that we all have to the universe. Trusting myself to be guided not by the mind chatter but by the quieter inner voice that had been silenced before is where my personal power comes from.

# PART 6: PASSING ON THE BATON OF HOPE

## *I Can and I Will - You Watch Me.*

The way we talk to ourselves creates the world around us.

For a long time I allowed the negative opinions of others to get inside my mind. Admittedly that was partly down to the way I had been treated BUT no matter how much I blamed others the responsibility to change it was mine and mine alone.

The choice is simple. Hold on to the past, keep all that resentment and bad feeling or decide you want different and set about creating different. You might not have created that negative voice in your head but allowing it to stay is sure as hell your choice. I chose to stop blaming and get on with changing.

The impact of choosing not to change that inner voice directly impacts the life we live. The most obvious example of this in my life wasn't that long ago.

November 2017 and I was blessed to be in Barbados in a mastermind for entrepreneurs that I could only dream of. The quality of the people in that room was outstanding, high achievers all with hearts filled with kindness. I, however, was feeling so down on myself that I blamed myself for everything. I was using language like, "I am horrendous". Yes, I was in a tough position but the mindset I had at that time lost me most of the opportunity that was in front of me.

Others in that group launched businesses due to their time there, launched a clothing line, created a business family. I at that time, just saw myself even more as the loser.

This was ALL created in my mind.

My negative self-talk might have been created by others, but I had the choice to choose that path and where that took me, which I did for a while and it took me to depression, losing my business and being a breath away from bankruptcy and homelessness.

I chose that path. I chose to keep telling myself those negative things each day. The outcome was 100% my responsibility and my choice.

However the choice to change that inner chatter was also mine to make. My daily mantra became: I can and I will - you watch me.

Each day, I committed to taking action to create a better future for my girls and I. I committed to saying, "I love you" to myself and my girls each day. I committed to saying, "I can change things, I will change things" and I was ready for them to watch me and learn that it can be done.

I set a 90-day time limit on seeing real results from it all and each day I set about reprogramming my mind with positive beliefs and Taking positive actions to reaffirm that and day by day creating our new world.

What we tell ourselves each day inside our mind creates our reality. Whether you choose to believe in the Law of Attraction, consciousness theory or simply that like attracts like I can promise you that when you believe good about yourself good things happen. When you believe negative about yourself you create that.

How do I know? Because from 2012-2014 I actively lived a life of positivity and gratitude. Late 2014 allowed myself to slip back into the negative conditioning of my childhood and I lost everything. The internal batterings I gave myself were also backed up by the people I chose to have around me at that time, without a doubt. However if I had held more self-belief and confidence it wouldn't have gone as far down as it did and I take total responsibility for that.

By choosing to tell myself positive things about myself each day. By choosing to take positive actions each day I am choosing to say I can and I will - just watch me.

I also made the conscious choice to only have other positive people around me going forward. If anyone doubted me, I remembered that is their own negative self-talk heading out towards me and kept going.

Choosing what I believe about myself is one of the biggest shifts in the outcome of my reality.

I decided who I am and wrote my list:

I am a loving, kind, fun and inspiring ,um who has a deep bond and respect with her daughters.

I am full of positive, happy, calm energy.

I am committed to following through daily on my life goals.

I am attracting supportive, high energy people who are achieving in life.

I am beautiful.

I am funny.

I am smart.

I am kind, thoughtful and giving but have healthy boundaries and have no need to heal others.

I am an author who has connected with the hearts and souls of millions.

I am healthy and fit.

I am fun, spontaneous and love life every day.

I am totally free from all past trauma and soul contracts.

I am forgiving anyone I perceive to have hurt me and thank them for the lesson.

I am a confident, efficient and successful businesswoman.

I am capable of greatness which can arrive in unexpected ways.

I am attracting the love of my life and ready for a healthy, fulfilling, committed relationship.

I am sexy, confident and able to shine brightly.

I am connected to source energy and able to allow that to flow through me.

I am trusting the universe to meet me in my actions and help me transform.

I am organised and on time.

I am worthy.

I am ready for miracles.

Taking control of the thoughts in my own mind and protecting that vision of myself and my reality was a huge change in the outcome of my life. I had this list everywhere around me. I wrote a copy in my bedroom, kitchen, bathroom, living room, I had a copy in my purse, a copy in my desk at work and if ever that negative chatter popped back up I would get it out and read it.

If someone else can poison your own mind against you, you can reprogramme it. What you tell yourself each day becomes your reality. What you believe about yourself becomes true. There is no way I would live the rest of my life believing what other people decided to tell me. I am the creator of my life and I want a different outcome to the one I am getting right now.

I take back the power for my own life. I stop looking to others to tell me what to do. I trust my own heart, my own light, my own intuition to get me there and I am ready to take action on these things every single day.

I chose to protect my goals for the future, my inner voice. I chose to protect it from anyone who couldn't see a brighter future for me.

It didn't mean that it was a walk in the park but it did mean that I took control over my own thoughts, my own reality and my own future. Adding in that 90 days allowed me to track my progress from where I was to where I want to get to.

Given that the mastermind in Barbados was the moment that I could see the direct impact of my inner voice causing me to miss opportunities I was amazed when writing this out that the end of that 90 days was to be the same weekend. I was invited back to meet with my mentor and this awesome team again. At the point of writing this I'd had to borrow money to feed my family, my day job was barely covering my bills and I am committed to making huge change.

I would deeply love to be back out in Barbados with that same group, this time celebrating my success. However to do that I must secure a better home for my family, clear my debts and be financially stable enough to make that trip to the other side of the world. Never say never, anything is possible when you are committed to finding the beauty from the trauma of the past. Let's see what magic swimming this moat has for me.

One thing I know for sure is: I can change my inner voice, I will create a fun-filled successful future for my family and you can watch me, or even better, you can join me.

## Your Lotus - Your Beauty - Your Story

We all have some form of mud in our lives. Some form of trauma, tragedy, pain, grief, shame. Whatever yours is it is as much a part of you as those days where you feel like you are winning at life.

Maybe your story makes mine look like a walk in the park, maybe your stuff doesn't feel as big as others but here is the thing, it is not a competition.

All of our pain, all of our suffering is big stuff to us. If you have never felt pain then I feel for you as I can promise you that once I was able to look beneath it all those parts of my life have been the biggest lessons.

Learning to love when I had never felt love actually made unconditional love so much easier. Learning to let go of my story of being a victim and not live in that place of shame, fear and guilt became as simple as taking off a coat, once I was ready.

Burying my feelings and always pretending to be "fine", "all good" or even more so "faking it" until I thought one day I would make it, was all part of my journey. My muddy moat lasted for around 37 years but every day I feel myself and my lotus bloom brighter and brighter because of that mud. It is an incredible feeling to have a sense of faith in the universe that I have learnt the hardest of my lessons and amazing things are on their way to me.

Your path may not be as muddy and murky as mine. But it doesn't mean you have any less right to bloom into your own lotus.

No Mud, No Lotus became my mantra through some pretty horrific times. Without those times, though, I would not have learnt the vast and wide lessons that I have. You can be taught something intellectually, read a book, study a class but to live through it, to feel that pain, to give a part of your story, your soul to it, then you are able to see into the eyes and soul of another with a deeper knowing. Have any of you dealt with a midwife who's never had a child, you can feel that she doesn't REALLY get it, can't you?

Many years ago I was a slimming consultant, having lost 6 ½ stone and I was blessed to be given the opportunity to help hundreds, maybe even thousands to lose weight and I could truly connect with them. Whereas when I met those who did similar, who had never swam the moat of being overweight, significantly overweight, never had to walk the path of emotional eating, I could feel that they knew the science but they had no idea of the heart of it.

By being able to understand when someone who desperately wanted to lose weight had gained that week, to be able to look them in the eye and tell them about the time I gained 10lb in a week took the shame, guilt and fear from them. Being able to lift the shame, guilt, fear of judgement from someone is a GIFT. The moment where someone no longer feels alone is a gift from your heart to theirs.

Your story can do that too. The crappiest times you have been through are where your beauty lies. It is not in your best days, the day you got the promotion at work, got married, had a baby; they are lovely but your beauty doesn't come from there.

Your beauty comes from the day you were so scared that your partner would end it with you that you had a totally irrational rant, the day you nearly quit your job because you didn't think you could do it. All those times you thought you were screwing up your life, those dark times, they are where your beauty and light will shine from.

Own your shit. Own it. It is as much a part of you as your glorious beauty. The moment you are able to own and share your shit, not just your shine, you will become even more beautiful. Even more real, whole, healed and help others do their work to sit with their darkness and heal too.

At my absolute worst I am the mum who was so scared of asking for help that I lost my shit on what is usually the most magical day of the year and I hurt my daughter. Nothing and no one could beat me up for that more than I have done for years. Feeling shame, guilt and pain didn't help my daughters. Owning that I was totally responsible for my actions, that I could have made a million different choices on the run up to that moment but I didn't, has always been my greatest strength.

Because at my absolute best I am also the mum whose daughters look at her with love, respect and a sense of fun, not fear, in their eyes. Because I have taught them that if they own their actions they can be anything they want to be. I am the person they trust with their darkest thoughts because I have shown them that the worst of me isn't all of me and doesn't take away from my good. They are able to have shitty moments and know I won't judge them for it.

I am not the worst of me. Nor am I the best of me. I am all of me. The good, the bad, the dark, the light and every glorious part in between.

You are also the whole of you. The amazing and the awful. Are you ready to own it, own it all and become the most whole and beautiful you have ever been?

Who are you at your absolute worst? What have you tried to bury or forget?

## I Am not my Mother

If there is one lesson I have had to learn the hard way it is this: I am not my Mother.

There are a million reasons why this is the case. There are moments where I see her in me, they are at the moments where I am at my worst. There can be no doubt about that. When I have lost my temper that is my mother coming out in me.

That does not make me like her, though. For if I was I would never have felt as awful as I did and looked for every way to get past that. I would never have taken total and unequivocal responsibility for my actions and I would have never got to know the worst of me.

I have lived in the shadow of my mother my whole life. I have lived in my own fear of becoming like her even more. I have put myself into that cage of fear and I have also faced the challenges to free myself from it.

The longer I am away from her the more and more I see it.

The longer I spend getting to know myself away from this fear of being like her the more I see it.

The more I forgive myself for ever going back to her once I was able to get away the more I see it.

The more and more I face stress, lack, strain and challenges but still keep my head and do not seek to blame others, play the victim or create drama around an already tough situation the more I see it.

Every time my girls look at me, laugh with me, share their thoughts with me, trust me I know I am nothing like my mother.

That is not to say I am the perfect mother. I know that I am not. I know that I have made mistakes. I know that I have caused pain. I also know I have never ever looked to blame my girls for that.

My girls are the best thing that have ever happened to me and I am proud that like me they choose not to blame the world or use their past as an excuse. They are kind to other children, they try hard and when they could say life has been hard for them they don't.

In facing my deepest fear and learning to let go of it and of any attachment to my mother I am allowing myself to grow in to the mum that I am naturally. A mum who values time over money, kindness over achievement, tolerance over judgement, respect over reward and knows that her children are only little for a while. I know that in a few short years they will choose where they spend their time. I do not ever want my children to feel obligated to see me. I want them to grow into women who want to see their mum.

You see, as I've previously mentioned, I believe that before we come to this earth for our human experience we choose all of this. I chose my parents. There were lessons I needed to learn from them both. My girls chose their parents too, both of us, for there are lessons their souls needed to learn.

When you are able to look beyond this one life and see it as souls living a human experience where we have come here to evolve and experience lessons, then it allows the lessons to be learnt faster. I have stopped trying to make things different. I have accepted that my mum is who she is and I chose her before I got here. As much as I am nothing like her, I am so grateful for the lessons she has taught me.

Much as with my father. I am grateful to him also. Although I have not seen him since I was 16 he has taught me that it can be easy to walk away. That parenthood for me isn't about being there when the going is easy. It is about being there, being consistent no matter what hurdles are put in your way. I am incredibly grateful for my dad choosing to go away and stay away because he taught me why it is so important that I have always remained in my girls' lives.

My girls know without a shadow of a doubt that I am here for them. They know that if they need me I would drop everything for them. They have seen me do it. They have watched me do it for others and they know I would do it for them. They know that there is nothing I wouldn't give for them. They also know that nothing material matters as much as them.

Time is our most valuable resource and I have given every moment of my time possible to my daughters and would do it all again in the blink of an eye. Now that I have been able to forgive myself, forgive my parents and accept that this has all happened because we all have lessons that we signed up for it is incredibly liberating.

Yes I was born to a woman who knows no feeling apart from rage. Yes I was born to a man who failed to protect me from her and ended up pushed out because of it. Yes I did some crazy things to get away from them both. Yes it has taken me over 20 years to get my head, heart and soul around it all but now that I am here. Now that I see the blessings in the lessons that living through the hell that was my parents I am so incredibly grateful.

There are so many children born to parents who shouldn't even have a dog, much less a child. It is not uncommon. It is bad enough that you have to live through that kind of hell which having parents like that is hell on earth, I know there are much worse than mine.

I know that mine were not the worst there can be. But what I can't stand is how when a child grows up they are taught to fear becoming like their abuser.

I am not my mother.

If you have lived with someone who didn't care for you, love you, protect you... you are not them. You are not to blame for it. No child is to blame for their parent and no adult from that kind of childhood should ever have to live in the shadow of the fear of becoming like their parent.

Any child who has lived through a life of abuse be it physical, mental, psychological, sexual, financial or, as in my experience, a mixture of many types has to realise they are not damaged, not broken, not to blame.

You are not them.

You are a darn warrior, You have made it out. Be proud of yourself. You are beautiful. Each of your scars is something to be proud of, it makes you unique. You have survived horrors you most likely don't want to tell another living soul. You have made it out alive.

Get as far away from them as you possibly can. Protect yourself. Learn to love yourself. Learn to see the awesome in the awful you have faced.

There is a beauty in coming through that, there is a beauty that cannot be taught it can only be lived through. There is darkness, of course you need to sit with, walk with, talk with your darkness and make it your friend. Once you can make friends with the darkness of your soul then they can never touch you again. You have all the power, all of the beauty and all of the grace.

You are not your abuser. You are a lotus ready to blossom. You can float on the top of the mud that has been your past, and shine with a beauty that can only be found in the souls who were born to face these lessons.

No Mud, No Lotus.

*******

### *Further Reading – the books that helped me.*

*Power Vs Force*, David R Hawkins, Hay House, 2002

*Letting Go,* David R Hawkins, Hay House, 2014

*Toxic Parents: Overcoming their hurtful legacy and reclaiming your life,* Susan Forward, Bantam, 2002

*The Empathy Trap: Understanding Antisocial personalities,* Dr Jane McGregor, Sheldon Press, 2013

*The Sociopath Next Door: The Ruthless Versus the rest of us,* Martha Stout, Tantor media, 2005

*Without Conscience: The disturbing world of the psychopaths among us* ,Robert D Hare, The Guildford Press, 1999

*The Buddhist Bootcamp,* Timber Hawkeye, Harper One, 2014

*The Emotionally Abusive Relationship: How to stop being abused and how to stop abusing,* Beverly Engel, Wiley, 2003

Each of these books have brought great insight however none did as much healing as giving myself the time, space and allowing to not be OK for a little while. Healing doesn't have to be pretty but if you want Love in your life then it is essential. No one can love you more than you love yourself and no matter who caused your lack of self-worth or life of fear it is your responsibility to learn to love all of you. You CAN do this, no matter what your past you are worthy of letting go and learning to Love!

If I can do this I know with every beat of my heart and the call of my soul that you can to. If you are unsure in any way borrow my total faith in you and love for you.

With much love,

Beccy xx